GOD'S PLAN FOR THE FAMILY

Love sex & Kids

GOD'S PLAN FOR THE FAMILY

Love Sex & Kids

CASEY TREAT

ISBN 1-57921-082-1
LCCN 97-062470

Published by
Christian Faith International
PO Box 98800
Seattle, WA 98198

Dedication

In 1978 when Wendy and I were married, a new family was birthed and the greatest part of my life began. Wendy proves the Scripture from Proverbs 18:22 to be true: **He who finds a wife finds a good thing, and obtains favor from the Lord.** She has meant more to me than anyone, other than Jesus. She has helped me grow, change, and be all that I can be. I'm sure I would not have accomplished what I have without her support and wisdom.

That's what is supposed to happen in God's plan for marriage. The husband and the wife are to lift each other to a higher place than they could ever go on their own. Marriage is not easy. It is definitely the hardest "project" I've ever undertaken, but it's also the most fulfilling and rewarding. I'm excited about the next eighty years with Wendy. If they are anything like the last twenty, it's going to be a great adventure.

Contents

Introduction

In 1980 Wendy and I started Christian Faith Center, and five years after that our first child was born: Caleb (1985). Then came Tasha (1987), and Micah (1989). I began my second greatest calling in life, that of being a father. Pastoring the church runs a distant third. I have learned so much while trying to be a good father. Today I know things about my Father God because of my relationship with my own children. Truly they are a **heritage from the Lord**, as Psalm 127:3 states.

The success of my marriage is my most important mission, followed by the success of my children, and then the success of my ministry. If my wife and kids are not cared for, God says I'm worse than an infidel. If my church is not cared for, God says I'm fired!

I have grown, suffered, been stretched to the limit, and blessed by my wife and kids, more than anything else in life. Someone has said, "It is easier to lead a nation than to lead a family." I would probably agree and add, "But family is more rewarding."

The union that God created between a man and a woman in marriage is an awesome thing. It is the first institution that God created and the only one He began besides the Church. The sharing of a life spiritually, emotionally, and physically is the ultimate fulfillment for men and women.

In Ephesians, chapter 5, Paul compares the marriage relationship to the relationship of Christ and the Church. If we mature in the marriage relationship as God teaches us, we will experience the best that life has to offer. It's not about money, careers, or the material wealth we acquire. It's about the most intimate and challenging relationship that can be experienced on earth.

When a person does not have a relationship with God, he is spiritually dead and separated from the spiritual life he longs for in his heart. When a marriage fails and a family experiences divorce, the same feeling of death and separation comes. An emotional or soulish death can be healed and restored, yet it never totally goes away. A scar always remains because man has separated what God brought together (Matthew 19:5,6).

One of the challenges of dealing with this subject is teaching truth without compromising, yet still loving and supporting those who have experienced divorce and family failures. I pray that you will value the truth that makes you free, yet at no time do I want you to feel condemned or put down. My goal is to lift you up and help you achieve God's perfect will in your family. You will feel conviction at times as you come across areas you need to change, but conviction is good. Condemnation paralyzes us in guilt and inferiority, while conviction moves us to grow and change. No one has done everything right. We are all growing and changing into the image of Jesus Christ.

Our society reflects the difficulty and the results of not building successful families. As the percentage of people getting divorced or never getting married climbs, the problems of abuse, crime, mental illness, and social dissatisfaction also increase. Some will say that my analysis is too simplistic and shallow, but the real issues of life are never hidden or deep. They are the simple truths of the Bible that everyone has known for centuries. They are the laws of God written on our hearts that we try to explain away with research data and social reformation, but they never change.

If a man is not faithful to his own wife, he will not be faithful to his boss, job, company, church, or anything else. If moms and dads don't train up their children in the way they should go, the rates of crime, divorce, unwanted babies, and unhappy people will continue to increase.

When families are healthy and strong, society is healthy and the nation is strong. The wall is built with bricks and if the bricks are crumbling, the wall will soon crumble too.

The good news of the truths presented in this book is that God has provided the tools and remedies to make families work and to fix family problems. I will share with you the practical and powerful truths that will enable anyone to have a great family. There is no one thing that will do it, but as you study the biblical insights in these pages, you will find the key thoughts that will help you and your family. As these truths are revealed to you, use them for yourself — not for your husband, your wife, or your children. You can't change them, but *you can give them an example to follow.* You can set the pace for a God-blessed family and soon the others will follow.

Singles, throughout *Love, Sex & Kids,* I will be sharing insights just for you. For those who have been married or have had children, I want to lift you to God's best for your life. The feeling of failure and loneliness does not have to control your life. God has a destiny for you.

In their religious fervor, some have preached divorce as the unpardonable sin and single parenthood as a struggle that never ends. Neither is true. God's grace and restoring power are much bigger than our failures. He forgives, heals, and restores, so we can go on in His path. He has not given up on you, so don't give up on yourself!

If you have not been married and do not have children, you have a clean canvas on which to paint a beautiful life. With God's plan in your heart and mind, you will see a wonderful world unfold before you. Let Him guide your brush and the picture will be beautiful. If you live the world's way, there will be some smudges and dark places that are not fun. But if you live God's way, you will go from glory to glory.

Value your single life and this time you have, to learn and grow. Protect your spirit, soul, and body. You don't need to go into family life with bruises or hurts. As you read, you will think of families you know. Watch and learn, but don't judge. It sounds so easy to be a husband, a wife, a mom, or a dad, but reality is very different.

Public schools give us a few months of special training to drive a car, but very few help us to prepare for marriage and family life. You are about to enter the next part of your marriage and family driver's training!

Casey Treat

God's Definition of "Family"

In the second chapter of Genesis, we find God's definition of *family*, what it is, and how it functions. Man does not decide what a family is, because God already defined it. We come along in our modern-day society and try to change what God said. By redefining family, we think it makes everything okay, makes people feel good, and makes society a happier place. Anytime we change what God has said, deny it, ignore it, or get away from His plan, we are going to suffer.

To understand God's definition of "family," let's look at Genesis, chapter 2, verses 18-25:

> And the Lord God said, "It is not good that man should be alone; I will make him a helper comparable to him." Out of the ground the Lord God formed every beast of the field and every bird of the air, and brought *them* to Adam to see what he would call them. And whatever Adam called each living creature, that *was* its name. So Adam gave names to all cattle, to the birds of the air, and to every beast of the field. But for Adam there was not found a helper comparable to him.

And the Lord God caused a deep sleep to fall on Adam [because He didn't want Adam to mess up His plan], and he slept; and He took one of his ribs, and closed the flesh in its place. Then the rib which the Lord God had taken from man He made into a woman, and He brought her to the man. And Adam said: "This is now bone of my bones and flesh of my flesh; she shall be called Woman, because she was taken out of Man." Therefore a man shall leave his father and mother and be joined to his wife, and they shall become one flesh. And they were both naked, the man and his wife, and were not ashamed.

God defines *family* as a husband (a male) and a wife (a female), with children being an addition to the "family." Until you understand the foundation of the family, you cannot build a successful family.

God defines *family* as a husband (a male) and a wife (a female), with children being an addition to the "family."

Wendy and I were married for seven years before we had any children. People regularly asked us, "Do you have children?" When we answered, "No," they asked, "When are you going to start your family?"

Man's perspective is, "Without children you don't have a family. You're just a husband and a wife." I wanted to ask, "What are we, just two people sleeping together? What if we choose never to have children? What if the Lord says, 'I want you to travel and minister all over the world, and you will not be able to have children?' Does that mean we can never be a family because we don't have kids?"

What about a husband and wife who, because of a physical condition, cannot have children? Are they not a family? The biblical perspective is that the family is made up of the husband and the wife, with *children being an addition to it.*

We had a family for seven years, and then we brought in a third member to our family, then a fourth, and then a fifth.

In Ephesians 5:31 Paul quotes from what we just read in Genesis 2:24: **"For this reason a man shall leave his father and mother and be joined to his wife, and the two shall become one flesh."** The two (man and woman) becoming one flesh (husband and wife) are a new family unit.

"For this reason a man shall leave his father and mother and be joined to his wife, and the two shall become one flesh," Ephesians 5:31.

Paul goes on to say:

> This is a great mystery, but I speak concerning Christ and the church. Nevertheless let each one of you in particular so love his own wife as himself, and let the wife *see* that she respects *her* husband.
>
> Ephesians 5:32,33

Verse 33 in *The Amplified Bible* says:

> However, let each man of you [without exception] love his wife as [being in a sense] his very own self;

and let the wife see that she respects *and* reverences her husband [that she notices him, regards him, honors him, prefers him, venerates, and esteems him; and that she defers to him, praises him, and loves and admires him exceedingly].

Then, Paul goes from "wives respecting their husbands" to:

> Children, obey your parents in the Lord, for this is right. *"Honor your father and mother,"* which is the first commandment with promise: *"that it may be well with you and you may live long on the earth."*
> And you, fathers, do not provoke your children to wrath, but bring them up in the training and admonition of the Lord.
>
> Ephesians 6:1-4

Notice, the husband is never to love his children as himself or even to love his children as Christ loved the Church. He is to teach them, train them, and bring them up in the training and admonition of the Lord, but he is not commanded to love them in the same way he is to love his wife.

Now, I think all of us Christian dads love our children as Jesus loved the Church. But my point is this: We were never commanded to do that. *We are commanded to love our wives like that.*

Many dads, if you really look at their behavior and attitude, are more committed to their kids than they are to their wives. Why? We go back to a lack of understanding about the definition of "family."

There are wives who dishonor their husbands, but they guard and protect their kids. This is a real issue in our society because we have become child-centered rather than

Bible-centered and Christ-centered, and we sacrifice marriages for children and wonder why the family is failing.

There are single parent families because of a breakdown in the family — not because God designed it that way. There are extended families. We can talk about grandparents, aunts and uncles and cousins and all that, but even that is not purely what God says *family* is.

The pure, focused, biblical definition of *family* is "husband and wife," and the kids become an addition to it. When the kids grow up and leave their family, they leave father and mother and birth a new family, a new one-flesh unit. And as their children grow up, they repeat the process. God's definition of *family* never changes.

We cannot change the definition of *family* by putting a new administration in the White House, or by taking a vote from society. I learned that lesson when I was five years old. If all the kids jump off a cliff, am I going to jump too? Your mom asks you that and you say, "But everybody is doing it!"

Society says that everybody is changing their perspective on relationships, sex, and family life, and on what a family is, so we should change the definition. You should have learned by the time you were five that just because everybody is doing something doesn't make it right.

Just because everybody is doing something doesn't make it right.

God established what the family and marriage relationship is all about and we are not called to change it. We can try, but we will end up with perversion. Truth that is changed is always a perversion, and perversion attracts problems. Big problems! As a result of not following God's plan for family, we are dealing with all kinds of hurts, pains, and problems. We need to get back to God's plan for the marriage and family, because that's where we will find His greatest blessings.

If your "family unit" does not fit God's description of *family*, there is no condemnation, judgment, put-down, naming, or blaming. But if we don't refocus on *family* as God describes it, the family is going to completely disintegrate.

Though we, as Christians, are quick to give verbal support to God's definition of *family*, some of us are not "living" out this description. We're still calling on Mommy and Daddy for help and approval. We're still living in the basement, or Mommy is living in the basement. You must *leave* so you can *cleave* to your mate. A whole lot of people aren't cleaving because they aren't leaving, so our families struggle.

In our world today, not only is there an attack on the definition of *family*, but there is an attack on the family unit itself. It is Satan's goal to destroy families.

Part of the agenda of the spirits of this world is to destroy the spiritual definition of *family*. Many of us are suffering because of that attack. We are struggling with divorce and with single parent families. We are trying to sort out what is going on in our lives.

There is forgiveness, restoration, healing, and a beautiful future ahead for you and your family!

Application of Family Covenant Truths

Please answer each of the following statements/questions, using Chapter 1 as your source of information:

1. "Family," as God defines it, is: _____

   _____

   _____

2. For my marriage to be successful, the husband is to _____ father and mother and be joined to his wife, and we are to become _____ _____ (See Genesis 2:24, Ephesians 5:31).

3. My marriage relationship will be patterned after Ephesians 5:33. The husband will _____ the wife as himself, and the wife will _____ her husband.

4. The scriptural principles I will follow to keep my family intact, as described in Ephesians 5:33 AMP, are:

   _____

   _____

   _____

   _____

   _____

   To me this means: _____

   _____

   _____

Securing the Family Foundation

The foundation stones of a successful family are knowing God, trusting Him, obeying Him, and loving Him. First, God is the center of the marriage when the husband and the wife *know* Him and each has a personal, intimate relationship with Him.

A successful family, like Adam and Eve, knows God. A wife who knows God recognizes His voice, communicates with Him on a regular basis (both talking and listening), and walks with Him. And a husband who knows God, who is born of His Spirit and filled with His Spirit, walks with God and communicates with Him.

If you don't know God, you don't have the foundation for success in your home. Before you get frustrated with your spouse's relationship with God, remember that the best way you can help your spouse to know God is to know Him more intimately yourself.

The best way you can help your spouse to know God is to know Him more intimately yourself.

Second, God is the center of a successful marriage and family when a husband and wife *trust Him*. To trust God means to put your faith and confidence in Him, knowing He will never let you down.

Many people know God in terms of a biblical understanding, and they are born of the Spirit, but they don't really trust Him. When they get sick, they run to the medicine cabinet. They trust their medicine more than they trust God.

Do you trust Him? Do you rely upon the Lord? Are you confident that He will come through with what you need? A successful marriage is one where both husband and wife put their *trust* in God. If the husband and wife aren't trusting God, they won't have a happy home, and that's where many marriages are struggling.

Wendy and I have found *trusting God* to be fun. Since we've been together, and really even before we got married, we were trusting God. In having our children, we trusted God. In building the church and our careers, our destiny, our ministry, we have trusted God. We never had a savings account or an inheritance or a family backing us that we could trust in. All we had was God, but He is more than enough.

Third, God is the center of a successful family when we *obey Him*. As long as Adam and Eve knew God, trusted Him, and obeyed Him, they lived in the Garden of Eden. They hung out with God in the cool of the day and lived in a perfect world.

There was sufficient water to keep everything green. They didn't need any clothes because the sun was blocked by a greenhouse of atmospheric control that kept the temperature constant and perfect. Sunburn was never a threat. They hung out in the Garden, named animals, and ate fruit. Everything was eternal and immortal. They just trusted God and obeyed Him.

There was only one tree — the tree of the knowledge of good and evil — that was restricted or "off limits" to them. They were commanded by God, **Of the tree of the knowledge of good and evil you shall not eat, for in the day that you eat of it you shall surely die** (Genesis 2:17).

A successful family is one that trusts and obeys God. If a husband doesn't tithe, he is disobedient to God. If you can't obey God, don't ask Him to bless your family, heal your kids, or prosper you on your job.

Let me just say something to the men. When we don't obey God, our wives do not trust us. Subconsciously, the wife looks to the husband to lead the family. She wants to submit to him as unto the Lord, because God put that desire in her. However, she cannot submit to a husband who disobeys God. I'd go as far as to say, that a lot of a wife's sexual hang-ups can come out of a lack of trust in her husband.

Fourth, God is the center of the successful family when a husband and wife *love Him*.

We do not love God because it is law, but we love Him out of a heart that is devoted to Him. God's commandments are not grievous. He hasn't put some heavy trip on us. He's the greatest Father, the greatest Leader, the greatest Creator. He is everything, and we can love Him and enjoy Him.

People who always look at the "have to's" and the negative side of obedience and discipline do so because they have no love for God. When you love your wife, it's easy to stay pure for her. When you love God, it's easy to walk with Him, obey Him, trust Him, and know Him. I'm not talking about religion, tradition, or law. I'm talking about a genuine love for God. A religious attitude about loving and obeying God will make you mean and ugly.

When you love God, it's easy to walk with Him, obey Him, trust Him, and know Him.

We're having a great time loving God, and consequently, obeying Him, trusting Him, and knowing Him. It's a positive thing, not a hard thing, to have a heart after God.

One of the things that scared me for years about having children of our own was seeing parents who had gone to church and who were good people, yet their kids ended up smoking pot, using drugs, fornicating, cheating, and lying. My confession and belief about kids at that time in my life was, "You never know how they are going to turn out." As I look back now, these parents were raising their kids by the "law" of the Word out of a religious attitude, but they didn't have a heart after God.

Kids grow up with the parents' heart, not just their head. If your heart, as a parent, isn't after God, then the heart of your children won't be after God either. So they go off and do their own thing.

Another thing about kids is they smell hypocrisy quicker than anybody. They can't explain it, but when they smell it, they run from it. This is why kids run out of the church at twelve, thirteen, or fourteen years of age, saying, "I don't want to go to church. I can't stand it."

If you know God, trust Him, obey Him, and love Him, you will have a great family — and your kids will be cool! They will be champion kids! Without these four elements, however, all the counseling, training, psychiatry, the forty-seven ways to have a happy kid, the twelve ways to raise a happy toddler, and the thirteen ways to have a good teenager, will be meaningless.

Without a relationship with God, faith in God, obedience to God, and a love for God, the family, more than likely, will fail.

Application of Family Covenant Truths

Please answer each of these statements/questions, using Chapter 2 as your source of information:

1. The best way I can help my spouse *know God* more intimately is: _____

   _____

   _____

2. I am learning to trust God by: _____

   _____

   _____

3. I am obedient to God by: _____

   _____

   _____

4. My love for God is revealed through: _____

   _____

   _____

   _____

Devaluing Marriage as a "Divine Institution"

The devil is at war with God's definition of marriage and His plan for the family. We see the demise of marriage in the increase of divorce, alternative lifestyles, or perverted lifestyles, and pain in our children.

Public schools tell teenagers it's all right to have sex using condoms. Instead of teaching their teenagers biblical family values, many parents tell their teenagers, "Sex is all right before marriage — just don't get a disease." In many cases, we fail to tell our teenage sons, "A young lady is a creation of God, and she may be the gift God has for you as a lifetime mate."

A young lady is a creation of God, and she may be the gift God has for you as a lifetime mate.

I believe the one thing that is causing so many families to disintegrate today is *not valuing the marriage as a divine institution*, or as the will of God. We have devalued marriage in our minds. We do not see the marriage relationship as a divine ordinance, a divine institution, something born of God. Man did not invent the relationship of marriage, God established it.

Genesis, chapter 2, verse 18, establishes this truth:

> **And the Lord God said, "It is not good that man should be alone; I will make him a helper comparable to him."**

It was God who said man should not be alone. So He made Adam a partner and brought them together. **Therefore a man shall leave his father and mother and be joined to his wife, and they shall become one flesh** (Genesis 2:24).

Marriage was not man's idea. And since it wasn't started by man and didn't come about by any evolutionary process, it can't be stopped or changed by man. Man comes along and says, "I can marry anybody I want to. I can marry another man if I want. I think I will marry my dog, or I could marry the cat." Or, a woman comes along and says, "I can marry another woman if I want to." Man didn't create marriage, so man can't change it. God said, **It is not good that man should be alone** (Genesis 2:18). But God didn't make him another man.

Man didn't create marriage, so man can't change it.

What happens is carnal man gets caught up in his flesh and in his emotions. One man said to me, "Pastor Treat,

I've never known love like I have with this man. I know that I am a homosexual because when I am around this man, I feel love that I don't feel from any woman. My feelings are real deep. How can it be wrong if it feels so right?"

The problem is that men and women, following their own thoughts and feelings, can be deceived very easily. Anytime you get away from what God said, you become deceived. You don't really know that you are deceived, but you are.

You think your new same-sex relationship is okay because it "feels" so good. I used to say that about smoking pot, thinking, "How can this be wrong when it feels so good?" Since all my old buddies are dead, I now say, "I was wrong." When we were snorting coke, we thought, "This is really good." We soon started seeing deaths, accidents, shootings, overdoses, and jail time. If you follow your thoughts and emotions, you can be deceived into thinking that anything is right.

We must get back to the Bible and God's definition of marriage and family. Some people today feel their marriage is no longer of God because they have found somebody else. "When I am with this other woman, I feel so good. Nobody has loved me like she loves me. Now I know that my first marriage was not of God."

Anytime you begin to ascertain the will of God by what you think or feel, you will probably be deceived. We've got to get back to a biblical perspective of marriage, and esteem that relationship as a "divine institution." Don't mess with it.

Anytime you begin to ascertain the will of God by what you think or feel, you will probably be deceived.

Years ago in a counseling session, I said to a couple who were experiencing difficulties in their marriage, "Marriage is born of God and your relationship is born of God." Without hesitation the woman blurted out, "This thing wasn't born in heaven, it was created in hell." That is how she felt with all the pain and problems she was going through.

Many people feel that their marriage is not of God. Then they begin to look back and try to find things to support their feelings: "When we first got together, I wasn't sure that I really wanted to marry him (or her) anyway. I did it because my mom wanted me to, and it seemed to be the right thing to do. I knew in my heart all along that it wasn't what God had for me, but we got married anyway."

Other people have said, "This marriage is not of God. When we got married, I didn't know what I was doing." There isn't anybody who ever got married who knew what they were doing! It's the same with having a baby. The woman goes to several months of classes, but when the baby starts to come, she says, "You didn't tell me this!" A better understanding doesn't come until you're in the delivery room, just as a better understanding of marriage doesn't come until you are in it.

Doubting or devaluing the marriage relationship opens the door for all kinds of compromise. Society tells us that it might be good for you to have an adulterous relationship, or to go to a topless joint, or to fantasize.

Doubting or devaluing the marriage relationship opens the door for all kinds of compromise.

I heard one psychiatrist say that "extramarital relation-ships" would bring life and romance back into the marriage. That's not true, but it will bring lies, fear, deception, mistrust, anger, hostility, resentment, bitterness, probably divorce, and possibly AIDS. When you pervert the truth, there will always be problems.

The fact that you "didn't know" going into the marriage what it would be like is no excuse to cheapen the relationship now by saying, "This marriage wasn't of God anyway." You don't have that option. There is no place in Scripture where God tells a man he has the wrong woman. Nowhere does God tell a woman that she has the wrong man. Marriage is a lifetime commitment.

___

Marriage is a lifetime commitment.

___

In our society, we have a time of dating, a process to get to know each other, like on a trial and error basis: "I'll try you on, go to dinner, try it for a while, and if it doesn't work, I will pass you off and find somebody else." You re-peat the process until you find someone you like, and then you get married.

What about the people in other cultures who are be-trothed by their parents? They can't say they didn't know what they were doing, because they were told who to marry.

In Bible days, the women wore veils so the men didn't even know what the woman looked like until they were married. They were expected to make their marriage work because marriage was considered a "divine institution."

If you view the marriage relationship as a divine institu-tion, born of God, then you can overcome every challenge that comes your way. But if you devalue the relationship, you will throw in the towel, give up, and walk away.

The beginning of death in a marriage is devaluing it by saying that it isn't really of God, that He has someone better for you, and that He will forgive you for bailing out. Once you start on that course, you have opened the door to a spirit of death in your relationship.

Marriage is a God-ordained relationship, so if you don't value it as such, don't enter into it.

Application of Family Covenant Truths

Please answer each of these statements/questions, using Chapter 3 as your source of information:

1. To me, valuing marriage as a "divine institution" means:

   _____
   _____
   _____
   _____

2. Perverseness comes into a sexual relationship by:

   _____
   _____
   _____

3. I am committed to increasing the value of my marriage relationship by:

   _____
   _____
   _____
   _____
   _____

4. One of the ways I have devalued my marriage relationship is by:

   _____
   _____
   _____

   I vow to change my actions and behavior by: _____

   _____
   _____

Marriage Killers

Before we look at the husband and wife's respective roles in the marriage relationship and ways to help the marriage grow and stay on track God's way, let's identify some of the marriage killers so we can eliminate them.

Selfish Ambitions and Desires

Death comes into many marriages because of self-centered ambitions and desires. Psalm 106:13 says, **They soon forgot His works; they did not wait for His counsel.** That means they wanted to do their own thing. They didn't want God's counsel, His plan, or His will.

Verse 14 says, **But lusted exceedingly in the wilderness, and tested God in the desert.** They lusted for "things," and their own desires were controlling their lives.

Verse 15 goes on to say, **And He gave them their request, but sent leanness into their soul.** Their own personal desires became their priorities: "Lord, I want this career, this house, these cars, that boat, the summer vacation, and the cabin." He says, "Your lusts are controlling your life, but I will give you what you want." Most people fail to realize that along with all of their desires, they are getting a lean soul. That means weak, shallow, immature, and quickly devoured by the devil. The animals that are eaten first in the jungle are the lean ones. You are a lean person, able to be gobbled up by the devil, when selfish ambition controls your life.

The wife may say, "I want a career. I am tired of these kids, and I need to be independent." So she gets her career, but she also gets leanness of soul. She starts liking the guy in the office next to hers, because he listens to her. (Please understand I am not against women with careers.)

In a marriage relationship, it is no longer what "you" want, it's what "we" want. It is no longer "my" desire, but "our" desires. When you have a family, it isn't "your" vision, it's "our" vision. You can have the things you desire, but it may cost you. You must guard against selfish ambitions and watch your personal desires, because when they become "yours" and not "ours," there's big trouble ahead. Death comes into a family relationship through selfish ambition.

Death comes into a family relationship through selfish ambition.

We live in a world where personal rights seem to be the main issue. We will sacrifice our kids or our marriage for our rights. We will sue people to protect our personal rights.

Recently, I dealt with a businessman whose company was being sued over a sexual harassment issue. A woman filed a lawsuit against a male employee who told a sexual joke in the office. The company didn't want to face the embarrassment and the costs that go along with such a suit, so the woman said she would drop the charges for a settlement of $50,000. The real issue wasn't that she felt sexually abused or harassed. She was willing to sacrifice her job, integrity, and relationships to get $50,000.

Should the guy have told the joke? No, someone should have slapped him upside the head! But then he probably would have sued for being slapped! Someone should have gone in and given an altar call, but of course that is unconstitutional in a public place. The problem is, everyone is focused on "what's in it for me?" We must guard against selfish ambitions and desires.

As a young pastor, my church went from a few members to thousands of members, and I realized I could do anything I wanted to do in terms of traveling, where I wanted to live, and what I wanted to drive. Within certain boundaries I could write my own ticket. God will give you the desires of your heart, but if they are selfish desires, you will probably end up with leanness of soul!

God will give you the desires of your heart, but if they are selfish desires, you will probably end up with leanness of soul!

Unforgiveness, Bitterness, Anger, and Resentment

Unforgiveness, bitterness, anger, and resentment are marriage killers. A couple can hold to a biblical commitment to stay together, yet hate each other. Bitterness, resentment, and sarcasm come out in the barbs and words aimed at each other.

Behind a feeling of embarrassment toward a spouse is bitterness, resentment, anger, and unforgiveness. You can think that you have forgiven and are free of resentment, yet still have something on the inside that makes you angry at your spouse. Maybe because they never gave you what they promised, they aren't who they said they would be, or they did something years ago that you are still angry and hurt about.

At one time I counseled a woman who had been married for fifty years who was still bitter because her husband had sex with her before they were married. She never forgave him for violating her before they were married. She didn't realize that was the reason for her attitude, her sarcastic words and put-downs. Through conversation and counseling, she finally recognized it as the root cause for her negativity.

We need to teach our young people that one reason you don't have sex before marriage is because if you violate the blood covenant of the sexual union, you breed mistrust into the relationship. That mistrust will continue on long after you say "I do."

One reason you don't have sex before marriage is because if you violate the blood covenant of the sexual union, you breed mistrust into the relationship.

Now, the public school or society isn't going to tell our young people that. Marriages are failing because no one is teaching the truth. Some of my police friends tell me how many calls they get each week because of domestic violence — husbands and wives knocking each other around because of anger, bitterness, and unforgiveness.

Hebrews, chapter 12, verse 14, says, **Pursue peace with all** *people*. *Pursue* means it is not automatic or natural. You don't get along with anybody naturally. You have to pursue a relationship and practice living in peace and harmony with other people, especially with your spouse. You have to do the same thing with other relationships. You can't have a good relationship sexually, emotionally, or mentally without pursuing it.

Nothing good happens automatically. Bad things happen without practice. Food rots if you do nothing to it. Clothes get wrinkled if you don't hang them up. If you want to keep them nice, you have to take care of them. A relationship will fall apart if you don't do anything to nurture it.

The writer of Hebrews says:

> **Pursue peace with all** *people*, **and holiness, without which no one will see the Lord: looking carefully lest anyone fall short of the grace of God; lest any root of bitterness springing up cause trouble, and by this many become defiled; lest there** *be* **any fornicator or profane person like Esau, who for one morsel of food sold his birthright.**
> **Hebrews 12:14-16**

Pursue peace with everyone and watch out for bitterness, because it will not only destroy you spiritually, it will defile you and keep you out of touch with God. Notice how the writer of Hebrews goes from bitterness right into fornication. In many cases, fornication follows bitterness.

A *root* is something under the surface. Bitterness is under the surface. We come to church, act nice, say the right things, but underneath there is a root growing. You could even be telling others the right thing to do in marriage, giving them good counsel and talking about all the godly things you know. But inside, a root of bitterness is growing and getting stronger. It is hard to pull up trees with deep roots.

If you have bitterness in you, it will not only defile you, but it will also defile others. How many people will sin because of your bitterness? How many lives will you defile? If I ever have a thought about messing up, that is one thought that stops me in my tracks. If I get mad while waiting for service at the store, trying to be my patient self and I want to say something so badly, I have to stop and ask myself, "How many lives will my temper affect?" Bitterness, resentment, anger, and unforgiveness are marriage killers.

Ungodly Associations

Ungodly relationships and associations will steal the life from a marriage. Of all the things I have mentioned, none of them make big, drastic changes immediately. But over a period of days, weeks, months, and years, they will destroy a marriage relationship.

In 2 Corinthians 6:14-18, Paul gives us wisdom for godly relationships:

> **Do not be unequally yoked together with unbelievers. For what fellowship has righteousness with lawlessness?**
>
> **And what communion has light with darkness? And what accord has Christ with Belial? Or what part has a believer with an unbeliever? And what agreement has the temple of God with idols? For you are the temple of the living God. As God has said, "*I will dwell in them and walk among them. I will be their God,***

and they shall be My people." Therefore, "Come out from among them and be separate, says the Lord. Do not touch what is unclean, and I will receive you. I will be a Father to you, and you shall be My sons and daughters, says the Lord Almighty."

"Don't be unequally yoked with unbelievers" also means anyone "acting" like an unbeliever.

Christian men often get in the flesh and let their hormones take over their brains. They can be worse than worldly men. Christianity isn't to blanket all of our behavior and allow us to go on with any relationship we want. You don't sleep with a guy just because he says he is a Christian. You aren't married to him. If you hang around ungodly relationships day after day, there will be great compromise in your godly standards for living.

Ask yourself, "Do my relationships build and strengthen, or detract from my marriage and family life?" When you listen to the negative counsel, jokes, comments, and attitudes of ungodly people, without realizing it you will take on the same spirit they have, and the Holy Spirit will back away from your life. We must watch who we hang out with.

I took all of the men who attend a monthly workshop at Christian Faith Center through a book about family and marriage. One of the things we learned is when a man begins to have an affair, it never starts out as "sex." Instead, *it always starts out as a friendship.* It could be with another Christian. In fact, many get together, talk about the Lord, read their Bibles, pray together, and share what they say they can't share with their spouse. Because this person tells them from their perspective how to deal with their spouse, they believe God put the relationship together. Adultery always starts as friendship, and ungodly relationships are destroying many marriages.

Ungodly relationships are destroying many marriages.

When our young daughters start getting their emotional fulfillment from their boyfriends, we have big trouble. Their emotional needs should be fulfilled by Mom and Dad, not by a boyfriend. So now you have an unequally yoked situation, with teenagers building a fire in their bodies.

When Satan came in the garden, he didn't come as a scary gorilla, a mean hippopotamus, or a bad dragon. He came as a smooth, subtle, soft serpent. The subtle things come in to destroy your life and family.

About twenty years ago, my friend Charlie came to school and said that his mom and dad had split up. I had never heard of it, and inside of me I was glad that would never happen to me.

A few years later, however, my parents split up. Now, over half of the kids in school, even in Christian schools, have parents who are split or remarried. In a few short years, what was unusual has become normal — not in God's eyes — but according to worldly statistics.

As a kid, I had heard about homosexuals, but I never knew anything about it. Now it is promoted as an "acceptable lifestyle" in America. In fact, if you do not agree with it and accept it, you seem to be the weirdo in the world's view.

Presently, laws are being written to deal with those who do not accept and promote homosexuality as a legitimate lifestyle. Churches may pay a price for preaching the Bible in this area, but we will live by conviction and not by convenience at Christian Faith Center. If the government says that you can't get a tax deduction because you are preaching against homosexuality, there will be some people who will change churches just to keep their tax deduction. These types of things are happening very quickly in our present-day society.

Hardness of Heart

In Matthew, chapter 19, verses 3-11, Jesus identified hardness of heart as a marriage killer.

> The Pharisees also came to Him [Jesus], testing Him, and saying to Him, "Is it lawful for a man to divorce his wife for *just* any reason?"
>
> And He answered and said to them, "Have you not read that He who made them at the beginning 'made them male and female,' and said, '*For this reason a man shall leave his father and mother and be joined to his wife, and the two shall become one flesh*'? So then, they are no longer two but one flesh. Therefore what God has joined together, let not man separate."
>
> They said to Him, "Why then did Moses command to give a certificate of divorce, and to put her away?"
>
> He said to them, "Moses, <u>because of the hardness of your hearts, permitted you to divorce your wives, but from the beginning it was not so</u>. And I say to you, whoever divorces his wife [or her husband], except for sexual immorality, and marries another, commits adultery; and whoever marries her who is divorced commits adultery."
>
> His disciples said to Him, "If such is the case of the man with *his* wife, it is better not to marry."
>
> But He said to them, "All cannot accept this saying, but only *those* to whom it has been given."
>
> Matthew 19:3-11

Jesus was pointing out that the reason for marriage failure is *hard hearts*. We can't blame it on our society, although it certainly has added to the problem. We can't blame it on our spouse, although they may be part of the issue. We can't blame it on our family and parents and other things around us. Jesus said the reason there is divorce is because of *hardness of heart*. And Jesus said divorce was allowed only because of sexual immorality. Divorce is never God's will, His plan, or His desire for any marriage.

Notice, Scripture doesn't say that divorce is the unpardonable sin, nor does it say that you'll be forever cursed if you have been divorced and remarried. But I want to emphasize, *marriage is a very sacred thing,* not to be taken lightly, not to be brushed aside with the whims and feelings of emotion of volatile humans. Marriage is not to be seen as something we can try and if it doesn't work, we can just get a divorce.

Marriage is a very sacred thing, **not to be taken lightly, not to be brushed aside with the whims and feelings of emotion of volatile humans.**

God sees the marriage relationship as a divine institution. In fact, the only thing that compares to the relationship of a man and a woman is the relationship with God and His people, the Church.

Application of Family Covenant Truths

Please answer each of these statements/questions, using Chapter 4 as your source of information:

1. My interpretation of "leanness of soul" in a marriage relationship is: _____

   _____

   _____

   _____

   _____

2. To replace "selfish ambition" in marriage, I would:

   _____

   _____

   _____

3. "What's in it for me?" in a marriage relationship is:

   _____

   _____

   _____

   _____

4. Name five of the "marriage killers" listed in this chapter:

   a. _____

   b. _____

   c. _____

   d. _____

   e. _____

5. Jesus identified the primary reason for divorce as
_____ of _____ .

To me, this means: _____
_____
_____
_____

The Husband's Role as "Priest" of His Family

> But I want you to know that the head of every man is Christ, the head of woman *is* man, and the head of Christ *is* God.
>
> 1 Corinthians 11:3

Paul is speaking of an authority system or a chain of command for families — God's corporate family as well as our individual families. He is not saying that God is more valuable and important than Christ, or that man is more valuable and important than woman. But he is saying that this is God's chain of command.

When we recognize God's chain of command, things will flow in an orderly manner and we will be blessed, but when we don't know this or we are out of order, unnecessary problems result.

Over the years, I've seen a lot of men who do not accept their role of headship or "priest" of their home and who shirk their responsibilities. They would rather watch a basketball game than play basketball with their kids. They would rather watch the television than spend time with their wife. They would rather just have sex rather than make the commitment to be a good husband. Therefore, we have a breakdown in the family, and the biggest price for it is being paid by our children.

Children who grow up without fathers are terribly handicapped. It doesn't mean they can't make it. But because of men who have shirked their responsibilities, women have picked up this spirit of trying to be something they are not: The "I am woman, hear me roar" spirit!

Women, will you allow your husbands to be the priest of the home? Husbands, will you take the responsibility for being a priest in your home? God did not hold Eve responsible for the sin in the garden. God judged Adam. Eve was deceived, but Adam knew better. It was because of Adam, not Eve, that sin came into the human race. If God was to judge the condition of the average American family today, He would not deal with the wife. He would not deal with the single mom. He would not talk to the mothers. But He would talk to the men and say, "You are the reason that your family is in this condition, because I called you to be the priest in your home."

If God was to judge the condition of the average American family today...He would talk to the men.

Under the Old Covenant, the priests represented the people to God and God to the people. They took the people's sacrifice and offered it up to the Lord. They took the praise, worship, and prayer and offered them up to the Lord. They were mediators in going to God for the family and from the Lord received direction, vision, and His plan for the family. The priest represented the family to God and God to the family. Any man who will accept this role will have a prosperous and blessed family.

I Peter 3:7 says, **Husbands, likewise, dwell with** *them* [your wives] **with understanding.** This means, understanding what God's plan is for your family. **Giving honor to the wife.** Do you honor your wife, or do you treat her like a nursemaid, a housekeeper, or a mother? Wives don't want to be their husband's mother. **Honor your wife as the weaker vessel**, not in terms of her abilities, but in terms of her irreplaceable value and her role in the family. Since the husband is the priest, he is to lead. **And as** *being* **heirs together of the grace of life, that your prayers may not be hindered.**

We must hear what God is saying. If we, as husbands, do not treat our wives right, our prayers will be hindered. Honor your wife, dwell with her with understanding, lest your prayers be hindered. Maybe you have been praying for a new job and you aren't getting it. Are you treating your wife right? You want God to bless your company, but perhaps He doesn't like the way you are treating His daughter.

If we, as husbands, do not treat our wives right, our prayers will be hindered.

My daughter is twelve years old now, and I am already thinking about when she turns sixteen. I am thinking what I am going to do *to* any young man who comes to see her. I have a plan. We will pray for about an hour, talk for a little while, and then we will see *if* they are going on a date.

Proverbs 18:22 says, *He who* finds a wife finds a good *thing* [a gift from the Father]. How do you think God feels when you take His gift and treat it like a housekeeper, or a sex partner without honor or understanding? God says, "Your prayers will be hindered."

I am convinced this is why some families can't get out of debt and are constantly struggling financially, yet the husband is working hard. God is saying to the husband who does not treat his wife as a gift, "Your career is cursed and your prayers are hindered."

I would be nervous if I were in that position, because there would be nothing to keep a drunk from slamming into your car on the freeway. There would be nothing to stop cancer from coming into your body. There would be nothing to stop a fire in your company. All of your prayers would be hindered. Don't get me wrong, you would still go to heaven, but you would probably get there faster than many of us!

God wants to prosper the man who is a priest in his home and who dwells with his wife according to knowledge and understanding.

What the Wife Needs From Her Husband

Here are seven things every woman wants and needs from her husband:

1. **Your wife wants to be loved.**

Love is expressed through affection, attention, communion, and communication. When you love your wife, you will talk to her without having the newspaper in your face. When you love your wife, you will spend as much time with her or more than you do with your buddies. Every wife wants and needs her husband to love her.

Love is a powerful thing. Scripture says that love covers a multitude of sins (1 Peter 4:8). It covers all kinds of challenges, so any problems you may have will seem insignificant when they are overshadowed with love. Without love to cover, however, problems in your marriage will become your focus.

I am convinced that the average marriage that breaks up does not have any problems that all other marriages don't have. It simply lacks the love to cover the problems. When Wendy and I have a disagreement, even in the midst of the battle, I recognize that love covers all the disagreements, misunderstandings, my weaknesses, and her weaknesses. We must understand that *love is a decision, a choice.* You don't fall in and out of love. If you don't choose to love, of course, you are not going to love.

2. **Your wife wants to be valued.**

Your wife wants to hear, "You are mine. There is no other." This is why the marriages in cults, where the husband has more than one wife, will never work. There is no way he can say to all twelve wives, "You are my one and only." This is why adultery and fornication are so disastrous and destructive. They plant seeds of doubt that are very hard to remove: "I am not the only one, and I'm not valuable and special. He could find another." It destroys the self-esteem, the identity, and the uniqueness of the wife.

This is the same problem with pornography and lust-filled movies and magazines. The person who involves himself in these areas really is saying, "*All* of these women make me feel good." Although the wife may never express it and you may never know it, she does not feel valued. Women should be the greatest fighters against pornography because they feel the brunt of men caught in it.

Even after living together for twenty, thirty, or fifty years, the wife needs to hear that she has fulfilled a plan, a purpose, and that she is valued and esteemed by her husband. Men, you must say it over and over with words, cards, flowers, your attention, and your time.

3. **Your wife wants security (spiritual and physical protection).**

My wife wants to know that I have spiritually covered our home, and that no devils, accidents, or evil are coming in. Spiritually and physically, I protect, watch, and guard my wife and children. I am not going to allow accidents and problems to come against us and hurt us.

If there are noises in the house, the husband should never say, "Honey, go see what's happening." He is to provide the protection. Don't send your wife out in a 1964 beat up Toyota with the doors falling off. Keep security around her. If men would give a little more attention to these types of things, it would make the sex life better. When you fulfill her needs, she is more eager to fulfill yours.

4. **Your wife wants friendship, which includes fun, recreation, and companionship.**

When you were dating, you went to the lake, and you rowed, walked, and hiked. You did things that were fun, then you got married. Now when you want to do fun things, the husband goes with the guys, and the wife goes with the girls. This is one way marriage gets torn apart. Find things you can enjoy and laugh about together as husband and wife.

The wife may not be too thrilled about going to world class wrestling night, but she may enjoy biking, tennis, racquetball, rowing, and hiking. Many guys spend more time having fun with their buddies than they do with their wife. Husbands, your wife needs friendship, recreation, and fun with *you*!

5. Your wife needs sexual fulfillment (romance or unity of the flesh).

In Genesis 2:24 God said of the husband and wife, **They shall become <u>one flesh</u>**. Most secular studies done today indicate that up to 75 percent of the women in America are not sexually fulfilled, which means that most men are not good lovers, not because they are not real men, but because they don't dwell with their wife with understanding.

The biggest sex organ in your body, men, is your brain and *how you think*. You have to understand your wife's body, her emotional needs, and how to help her to be sexually fulfilled. Your physical body is not your problem, and you can meet your wife's sexual needs if you understand.

There are women who have decided they will never be sexually fulfilled, so they "do their duty" and leave it at that. Those kinds of feelings are hurtful and intimidating to the man. So women, instead of accepting that attitude, you can desire God's best and help your husband understand you.

God commands a husband and wife to have good sex:

> Rejoice with the wife of your youth . . . Let her breasts satisfy you at all times; and always be enraptured with her love.
>
> Proverbs 5:18,19

6. Your wife needs direction and leadership, a vision and a future.

The husband should provide the vision and the future. In far too many families, divorce occurs when the children reach eighteen. The vision ends there, and where there is no vision for the marriage, it perishes.

Your vision should go beyond this point to, "What are we going to be as a couple when we are sixty-five?"

7. **Your wife needs provision and financial security.**

Many wives go to work, although they really don't want to, because the husband is not able to bring in the finances that the family needs. With a difficult economy and a society that has devalued the marriage, both husband and wife work in many cases.

The husband should still do his best to lead the home financially, manage the money wisely, and give the family financial security. Husbands, God not only said to take care of your wife and kids, but to leave an inheritance for your grandkids. **A good *man* leaves an inheritance to his children's children** (Proverbs 13:22).

Since God told us to do it, it is possible to do it. God would never give us a command that we couldn't fulfill, because He is just. So if we follow His plan, it is possible to not only provide wealth for our children, but also for our children's children.

In the next chapter, we'll look at the woman's role in the home and what the husband needs from his wife.

Application of Family Covenant Truths

Please answer each of these statements/questions using Chapter 5 as your source of information:

1. God's chain of command given in I Corinthians 11:3 is:

   _____

   _____

   _____

   _____

2. The husband's role as "priest" of his family means:

   _____

   _____

   _____

   _____

3. Prayer is hindered when: _____

   _____

   _____

4. The seven things a wife needs and wants from her husband are:

   a. _____

   b. _____

   c. _____

   d. _____

   e. _____

   f. _____

   g. _____

The Woman's Role
in the Home

In understanding what the husband needs and wants from his wife, let's first read two foundational Scriptures:

> Who can find a virtuous wife? For her worth *is* far above rubies. The heart of her husband safely trusts her; so he will have no lack of gain. She does him good and not evil all the days of her life. She seeks wool and flax, and willingly works with her hands. She is like the merchant ships, she brings her food from afar. She also rises while it is yet night, and provides food for her household, and a portion for her maidservants. She considers a field and buys it; from her profits she plants a vineyard. She girds herself with strength, and strengthens her arms. She perceives that her merchandise *is* good, and her lamp does not go out by night. She stretches out her hands to the distaff, and her hand holds the spindle. She extends her hand to the poor, yes, she reaches out her hands to the needy. She is not afraid of snow for her household, for all her household *is* clothed with scarlet. She makes tapestry for

herself; her clothing *is* fine linen and purple. Her husband is known in the gates, when he sits among the elders of the land. She makes linen garments and sells *them*, and supplies sashes for the merchants. Strength and honor *are* her clothing; she shall rejoice in time to come. She opens her mouth with wisdom, and on her tongue *is* the law of kindness. She watches over the ways of her household, and does not eat the bread of idleness.   Her children rise up and call her blessed; her husband *also*, and he praises her: "Many daughters have done well, but you excel them all."

Proverbs 31:10-29

Wives, likewise, *be* submissive to your own husbands, that even if some do not obey the word, they, without a word, may be won by the conduct of their wives, when they observe your chaste conduct *accompanied* by fear. Do not let your adornment be *merely* outward — arranging the hair, wearing gold, or putting on *fine* apparel — rather *let it be* the hidden person of the heart, with the incorruptible *beauty* of a gentle and quiet spirit, which is very precious in the sight of God. For in this manner, in former times, the holy women who trusted in God also adorned themselves, being submissive to their own husbands, as Sarah obeyed Abraham, calling him lord, whose daughters you are if you do good and are not afraid with any terror.

Husbands, likewise, dwell with *them* with understanding, giving honor to the wife, as to the weaker vessel, and as *being* heirs together of the grace of life, that your prayers may not be hindered.

1 Peter 3:1-7

I believe these two scriptural accounts give us an accurate biblical balance of the perception we must have for the role of Christian women. The world would have us think that a good, Christian woman is weak, quiet, withdrawn, barefoot, pregnant, and busy in the kitchen. The world, of course, reacts against this stereotype. Their deception of Christian women is that they can't wear makeup or nice clothes, but they must stay at home and be submitted to their husband.

The devil has convinced the world that Christian women are going to have a bad time and has deceived men to believe this is what God wants. Nothing could be further from the truth. The Proverbs 31 woman is one busy lady. She is a businesswoman, a manager, a leader, and an organizer. She is a very powerful woman. To live up to this description of a woman, you must have the power of God.

The Proverbs 31 woman is one busy lady. She is a businesswoman, a manager, a leader, and an organizer. She is a very powerful woman.

On the other side of the coin, she also allows her husband to be very powerful by submitting to him and allowing him to be the man God called him to be. So, for the Christian husband and wife, there is strength and security, not competition. The feminist movement, on the contrary, is backed by a very competitive spirit which says, "I'm as good as, or better than." They have missed the whole point. First, to even compete with someone, you lower yourself.

When a woman says, "I'm as good or better than a man," or a man says, "I'm better than a woman," both lower themselves by entering into comparisons and competition that are irrelevant to who they are as individuals in God's sight.

God is saying that instead of competing with each other, *we are to complete one another.*

If we will keep the biblical perspective, both husband and wife will live happy, fulfilled, successful lives, and they won't have to degrade anyone to do it. And if we'll keep God's perspective, both husband and wife will *rise to their highest possible level of potential in life!*

On the one hand, the Proverbs 31 woman is busy, she has employees working for her in her house, and she is a mighty businesswoman, not just taking care of the clothing of her kids, but buying and selling real estate. (Now, as a woman, you may not be a realtor, but what this is saying is, *you are a woman of wisdom and great ability.*) Yet, she submits to her husband and allows him to be the priest of the home. She loves her husband and influences him more by what she does than by what she says.

In verse 1 of 1 Peter, chapter 3, God says the wife will win her husband by her conduct, *not* by her words. I am convinced that women preach louder when the mouth is shut.

When I see my wife busy dealing with issues that I know I should be doing, and handling things that I know I should be aware of, then I get convicted and I get busy! When a wife talks to you about something you, the husband, have failed to do, it's like, "Okay, okay, okay." But when she acts right, it's like, "Oh, man, now I'm convicted." The verse that says the wife wins her husband by her conduct is so true. Wives, you need to realize the great influence you have, and that *it's more with conduct than with words.*

I know some situations where Christian wives have been trying to get their husbands saved, and from my perspective, the only reason the guy isn't saved is because of his wife. If she would be quiet, he'd get saved in a heartbeat.

But he's resisting because he knows if he ever comes to church, she's going to say, "I told you so." She's going to blab and embarrass him in front of everybody: "This is my husband. I've been praying for him for thirty-seven years."

He's been trying to figure out a way to get saved without her knowing! He wants to serve God, but he doesn't want to be condemned by his wife. Women, win him with your conduct, not with your words!

What the Husband Needs From His Wife

Here are seven things a husband wants and needs from his wife, in a sequence of priority as I sense they should be:

1.   **The husband wants and needs encouragement from his wife.**

Every man wants and needs his wife to be a cheerleader, to believe in him, even when he doesn't believe in himself.

Wives, when your husband is down, he comes home feeling bad, and he's doubting himself, you have such authority and ability to say, "Honey, you're the best. You can do it. I know it's going to work. I have confidence you're going to make it happen. I'm not worried."

If your husband loses his job, you can say, "Kick them in the knee! Rah! Rah! Rah! Kick them in the other knee. Two bits, four bits, six bits, a dollar. You can get a better job tomorrow!!" The wife who is her husband's cheerleader helps him believe in himself.

The wife who is her husband's cheerleader helps him believe in himself.

Wendy continually encourages me and says, "Hey, it's all right. You're doing it. You're on course. You're the guy. You can handle it!" Because she believes in me, I have been able to go further than I ever would go by myself. I'm convinced, although most men wouldn't admit it, that we need wives who will encourage us and be cheerleaders who believe in us.

This is why one of the tools of the enemy is to get the wife to focus on the faults of her husband. The enemy wants to blind the mind so all you can see are the faults and weaknesses in your husband. The enemy does that, because he knows if you keep talking about what's wrong with him, he will soon leave. Either in his heart or physically, he will separate himself, because a man needs an encourager, not someone to remind him of how "out of it" he is.

As men, we know when we're "out of it." We know when we've missed it. We know when we have faults and weaknesses. Whether we admit them or not, we are aware of them. When the wife is focused on our weaknesses and reminds us of them, and we're already down, we say, "Why do I need her? I mean, who needs the devil with a wife like that? I go to work and I've got the devil on me trying to defeat me, and I come home and she reminds me of everything that's wrong." She says, totally insensitive to his feelings and needs, "You are fifteen minutes late. The dinner is cold as usual. If your head wasn't screwed on, you'd forget it, too!" And on and on and on....

The put-downs and discouragement begin to weigh on the husband, and he acts tough, but he is hurt, even though he may act as if he didn't hear it.

If the wife keeps "walking on him" with her negative words, even though he may be acting a little flaky, here's what usually happens. Next morning he goes to the office and his secretary says, "Boy, do you look sharp today!" He hasn't had any praise for days, and the secretary goes on, lays a file down on his desk, and says, "I really like the way you handled that case yesterday." He's thinking, "I've got a cheerleader here. I haven't had a cheerleader in months."

The next day on his way out the door to go to work, he hears, "What time are you going to be home? Late again, I suppose? It's been a long time since you spent any time with me and the kids, and we're getting sick and tired of it."

He walks into his office and his secretary says, "A new tie? My, you dress sharp." He has to weigh who he likes more. He knows who he loves, but he's checking out who he likes.

Wives, you need to be an encourager, a cheerleader, and I guarantee, your husband will focus on the good things you desire if you will focus on his positive attributes rather than amplifying the negative. He may act tough like he doesn't need encouragement and approval, but he does.

Wives...your husband will focus on the good things you desire if you will focus on his positive attributes rather than amplifying the negative.

Men need wives who will lift, build, and encourage. I believe this is man's number one need, and if the enemy can get the wife focusing on the negative — whining, complaining, and griping — divorce seeds are being planted. This is one reason men are finding women in the world. I'm certainly not excusing it or condoning it, I'm just explaining.

The reason they pick women in the world is because they say nice things that they are not hearing at home.

2. **The husband wants and needs his wife to be sexually open and free with him.**

In terms of the average Christian home, the world believes Christians aren't supposed to be beautiful and sexually active. That's because Hollywood doesn't know the truth. The sexual revolution has not brought freedom to people in the world. Instead, it has brought hurt, pain, and bondage. The average person in the world is not sexually free.

The majority of women are not sexually fulfilled on a regular basis, and more than half the men in America are not sexually fulfilled. We don't need a sexual revolution as the world portrays it. We need to go back to the Word, go back to God's plan. God set up a way for the husband and wife to be one flesh, sexually united, and in that sexual union, there is fulfillment for both of them.

The sexual relationship of the husband and the wife is a primary part of success in marriage. Christian men want their wife to be sexually and physically open and free. That includes being physically attractive. We don't want our wives to try to live up to some Hollywood or pin-up girl standard. Christian men, as a whole, don't want their wives to be some kind of glamour queen, but they do want their wives to be pretty and sharp, to take care of themselves, to look good and smell good. To be sexually and physically attractive is an important part of the marriage relationship.

The sexual relationship of the husband and the wife is a primary part of success in marriage.

God made human beings with bodies, and we are to be stewards of the body. When God made animals, he put feathers in certain places to attract the opposite sex. He put big manes on some of them to attract the opposite sex. Birds know how to put on their dance and show their stuff. Likewise, God made our bodies in a certain way and He put certain things in certain places to attract the opposite sex. *The Lord did it!*

The husband wants his wife to be aggressive and open. The Bible says that Adam and Eve were both naked and were not ashamed. She did not run from the bathroom to the bedroom with her bathrobe on and slip under the covers and throw out her bathrobe. She didn't say, "Turn the lights out!" There was an openness, a freedom, and a liberty in their sexual relationship, and men need that.

I don't want to come across carnal or negative in any way, but I am saying to the Christian ladies, your man needs a free, open, aggressive, and fun sexual relationship with you. If you don't give it to him, he's got two options: He's either going to dream one up and fantasize about it, or he's going to find someone else. I'm not excusing his behavior or saying it's right. But let's plug in to what is happening in the real world and let's have God's will in our homes. *The wife who meets her husband's needs won't find him going anywhere else to get his needs met.*

The wife who meets her husband's needs won't find him going anywhere else to get his needs met.

---

3. **Every man wants and needs his wife to be intelligent, a communicator, and aware of the issues of this life.**

Men don't want their wives to be spaced out and unaware of what is going on. "Gosh, honey, I didn't know the credit card was already at its max." Come on, no man wants a dingy wife! Wives should be able to discuss the issues of life with their husbands.

The Proverbs 31 woman was an intelligent woman. She ran businesses and managed employees. She made her husband proud. The Bible says he was exalted in authority with the other elders because of his relationship with his wife. An intelligent wife always raises the standard of the home.

Now, I'm not saying the wife should be in any particular business. I'm not saying she should be home or be in the workplace. I'm just saying she should be alert, sharp, intelligent, aware, and able to discuss and communicate about the issues of life. In this way, she will also help the children to rise up with the ability to handle the issues of life without fear or trepidation.

4. **Every husband wants his wife to be disciplined, a manager of the family, organized, and in control financially.**

The Proverbs 31 woman managed her home. Wendy manages our home in many areas. Your home may be different, depending on whether you have two people working, what those jobs are, and what your schedules are. But to whatever degree it balances and works, men need wives who can coordinate and stay plugged in to what's happening.

I tend to get my schedule so full that Wendy has to remind me and help me bring it into balance. It's better for the wife to help the husband manage than to complain. He probably doesn't even know what his schedule is. I always rely on the Scripture in Matthew, chapter 6, verse 34, **Do**

not worry about tomorrow. But I thank God Wendy takes thought for tomorrow! She helps me stay on top and stay plugged in to what is happening.

There are times when Wendy goes through our financial budget of expenditures in the home, and she says, "We've been spending too much money in this area, or that area," and we make adjustments. She maximizes our dollars in the home. Women need to rise up and be leaders and managers in the home and get the home budget in order.

In our house, I manage the investments, the real estate purchases, the children's future accounts, the college accounts and those kinds of things. Wendy manages the home expenditures and oversees how the money is spent and what we do in the home. We work together, and I enjoy having a disciplined wife.

The "old" stereotype of the wife is the woman who goes to the mall, spends a bunch of money, and maxes out the credit cards until plastic surgery is needed (cutting up the credit cards)! The "new" picture of the godly wife is one who manages, leads, organizes, and keeps the home in order. First Corinthians 14:40 says, **Let all things be done decently and in order.** Although this chapter deals specifically with the spiritual gifts, I believe this principle also applies to the home.

Discipline also has to do with the appearance of the home. It's not all the wife's responsibility, but she can help manage the appearance of the home. If I come to your house unannounced and you would be embarrassed about the condition of your home, then you've got problems. Any day, every day, anybody should be able to step in, not that it will always be perfect, but we need to be good, disciplined leaders of our homes.

5. **Every husband needs and wants a secure helpmate.**
The Bible says that God created the woman and brought her to the man as his helpmate or "helper" (Genesis 2:18). Some women work outside the home by choice, others because of need, and others work in the home with the children and the family business. There is no good or bad. It's a personal choice depending on your needs and circumstances. Whatever way it is handled in your home, the husband needs his wife to be a secure helpmate.

If the husband feels like the wife is always looking for some way to find fulfillment, he may never admit it, but he is hurt. If the wife takes the position, "Well, I do this little house stuff and the kid stuff, but I really live for my job," the husband may see himself as number three on the totem pole: "There is the job, the kids, and then me."

Since the wife is looking somewhere else for fulfillment, the husband's assumption is that he and the children are not enough to fulfill her life. He may never express his feelings, but I guarantee you, the man feels bad if that's the case. The wife may be working, but she needs to communicate and feel a security in her role as a helpmate in the home and in the marriage.

6. **The husband wants and needs his wife to be willing to have some fun and participate in recreational activities, particularly on his days off.**
On their day off, I know many couples who go in different directions. That may happen at times because of needs of the home, but the majority of your time away from the career, away from the office, should be *with each other*. I know many men who are frustrated with their wife because she won't participate. "I don't want to do that. You go ahead, honey. I'm going to go shopping." Or, "I'm going to stay home." Or, "I'm going to go out with the girls."

The husband doesn't want the wife to compete, and he doesn't need her to be as good as he is. He just wants her to participate so they can have some fun together. Men tend to be more activity prone, and women more relationship prone, but the wife can still participate.

Women, go to the gym with your husband, put on your shorts, and just get involved. "I don't want to lift weights." Well, just stand there and do jumping jacks while he lifts weights. "I don't like golf." Then carry his bag around and tell him everything you've always wanted to tell him. Participate! Get involved!

Wendy and I like to ride bikes. She can't ride as fast or as far as I can, but if we can just make it to the next espresso stand, it will be all right! We have a good time. It doesn't matter how fast we go or how far we go, we're just out there to participate with each other, have a good time, and have some fun together.

Many couples are missing out. You're thirty, thirty-five, forty, or fifty years old, and you're not having any fun together. Find something you can do together. Go dig worms. Chase snakes. Ride bikes. Play golf. Climb mountains. Swim. Do something! You can participate and have fun together.

7. **Every husband wants and needs his wife to be a good homemaker.**

Now, I didn't say a "housecleaner." I said a good "homemaker." Have you ever seen a single man's house? It may be the neatest place in town, organized with everything in place, or it may be a dump, but it's not a home. It's a house. It's a pad. Women have the ability to make a house into a home. That has to do with decor, activity, and relationship.

Every man wants his wife to make the house a home, whether she works or not. If they have children, he wants his wife to be a good mother, not one of the moms down at the mall jerking the kids by their arms or screaming, "You kids are driving me crazy!"

I'm convinced that wives have more influence than they may ever know, and they are missing their opportunity when they influence in a negative way rather than using their godly talents to affect positive change.

Application of Family Covenant Truths

Please answer each of these statements/questions using Chapter 6 as your source of information:

1. Name six of the qualities of a Proverbs 31 virtuous woman:

    a. _____

    b. _____

    c. _____

    d. _____

    e. _____

    f. _____

2. The words of the Proverbs 31 virtuous woman are filled with _____ and _____ _____ (v. 26).

3. According to 1 Peter 3:7, a husband and wife's prayers are hindered by: _____

    _____

    _____

4. Peter says the husband, even if he doesn't obey the Word, can be won by the conduct of his wife. To me this means:

    _____

    _____

    _____

5. I do not want a "competitive" spirit in any area of my life because: _____

_____

_____

_____

6. To rise to my highest level of potential in life, I will:

_____

_____

_____

_____

7. Seven things a husband needs from his wife are:

a. _____
b. _____
c. _____
d. _____
e. _____
f. _____
g. _____

The Sacredness of Virginity

I n the Old Testament we are dealing with an age that
was ruled by law, and in the New Testament we are living in an age of grace. The principles and truths about a
godly marriage relationship in both the Old and New Tes-
taments, however, remain the same. The things God de-
manded of people in the Old Testament, He still demands
today, but the judgment is different because we're under
the grace of the Lord Jesus Christ. We have forgiveness and
mercy, but in the Old Testament the law prevailed.

Deuteronomy, chapter 22, verses 13-15 say:

> "**If any man takes a wife, and goes in to her** [has
> sex with her], **and detests her, and charges her with
> shameful conduct, and brings a bad name on her, and
> says, 'I took this woman, and when I came to her I
> found she was not a virgin,' then the father and mother
> of the young woman shall take and bring out the *evi-
> dence* of the young woman's virginity to the elders of
> the city at the gate"** [or at the place of authority].

To give evidence of virginity, a linen cloth was laid on the marriage bed the night the couple had sex for the first time. The father provided the cloth for his daughter. When a virgin has sex, the hymen is broken and bleeding results. A blood covenant is made between the man and the woman. Virginity is sacred to God because the husband and wife are establishing a lifelong blood covenant.

Virginity is sacred to God because the husband and wife are establishing a lifelong blood covenant.

If you gave your virginity to some other man that you had no commitment with and now you are lying with the man you are establishing a lifetime commitment with, you have given up the opportunity to establish the blood covenant and there is no evidence of virginity. What about the man who has gone off with other women and now he has found the woman to whom he wants to commit his life? He cannot establish the blood covenant because he is not a virgin. He has removed the potential to start the marriage covenant the way that God wanted it to be established.

I don't want this to sound condemning because many Christians have come out of the world where they have had sex or they have been married before and now they are building their lives with Christ at the center. God forgives, cleanses, and restores, but the fact of the matter is, though spiritually you may be a virgin, physically you can never get your purity back. This is why we say to our young people, "Don't give it away."

I have never yet met a person who said, "I'm so sorry that I was a virgin when I got married." However, I have met husbands who have said, "I'm sorry I wasn't a virgin when I got married, because I'm still trying to deal with the problems and feelings that I created because of having sex before marriage."

In the Old Covenant, when the husband detested his wife and said, "She's not a virgin, I don't want her," the girl and her father were to bring the cloth before the city elders to prove or disprove her virginity.

Verses 17-19 of Deuteronomy, chapter 22, say:

> 'Now he has charged her with shameful conduct, saying, "I found your daughter was not a virgin," and yet these are the evidences of my daughter's virginity.' And they shall spread the cloth before the elders of the city.
>
> Then the elders of that city shall take that man and punish him; and they shall fine him one hundred *shekels* of silver and give *them* to the father of the young woman, because he has brought a bad name on a virgin of Israel. And she shall be his wife; he cannot divorce her all his days.

In Old Testament days, they didn't say, "Gosh, you guys are off to a bad start. I can tell right now, this marriage is going to be tough. You might as well throw in the towel and get a divorce." Instead, the elders sent him back home and said, "Get back in that house and love this woman and treat her like your wife. You cannot divorce her." How would you like to be in that house that night when the husband says, "Sorry, honey, for lying about you and trying to dump you"? The point is, they were to deal with it, overcome it, and go on with the marriage.

Verses 20-21 say:

> "But if the thing is true, *and evidences* of virginity are not found for the young woman, then they shall bring out the young woman to the door of her father's house, and the men of her city shall stone her to death with stones, because she has done a disgraceful thing in Israel, to play the harlot in her father's house. So you shall put away the evil from among you."

Thank God we don't live under the Old Testament law. The judgment has changed, but the principles are still the same. God is saying, "You are involved with evil when you have sex before you are married." He doesn't call it "an affair." He doesn't call it "having fun." He doesn't call it a "sexual revolution." He calls it <u>evil</u>, and He says it needs to be put out of your city. This is true for men as well as for women.

Verse 22 goes on to say, "**If a man is found lying with a woman married to a husband, then both of them shall die.**" I think this would put a curb on adultery! Think about it. Under the Old Covenant, if Bob and Jane have been sleeping around, committing adultery, and they are caught, they are dead. We would go to their funerals!

In our society, we've made it such a light offense. The psychiatrist says it puts zest back into your life. The world says it's normal. Everyone tries to promote it as, "I didn't plan it, it just happened."

Under the age of grace, which we are in, both would be forgiven and restored. But the principle of the Old Covenant and the New is the same: Adultery is wrong. It's not an affair, it's adultery. It's sin!

> "If a young woman *who* is a virgin is betrothed to a husband, and a man finds her in the city and lies with her, then you shall bring them both out to the gate of that city, and you shall stone them to death with stones,

the young woman because she did not cry out in the city, and the man because he humbled his neighbor's wife; so you shall put away the evil from among you.

But if a man finds a betrothed young woman in the countryside, and the man forces her and lies with her, then only the man who lay with her shall die."

Deuteronomy 22:23-25

I believe that would slow down the rape problem, too! Verses 26 and 27 go on to say:

"But you shall do nothing to the young woman; *there is* in the young woman no sin *deserving* of death, for just as when a man rises against his neighbor and kills him, even so *is* this matter. For he found her in the countryside, *and* the betrothed young woman cried out, but *there* was no one to save her.

The Old Covenant principle is, if a man and a woman are having sex outside of marriage, both of them die. But if a man rapes a woman and she cries out and tries to fight and stop him, then the man dies because there was no one there to help her. The point God is making is sex is sacred. Don't play or party with your sex life, but recognize it as a gift from God, dedicated to one person with whom you make a lifetime covenant.

___

Sex is a gift from God, dedicated to one person with whom you make a lifetime covenant.

___

Our public schools and our society have made sex a mockery, a joke, and a game, and they wonder why disease

81

is rampant and divorce is increasing. They wonder why the boys get together and have contests to see how many sexual conquests they can get. What else should we expect if we're giving them condoms? Yet society says, "We're trying to protect them." If our motive is "protection," we should be telling them what God says about sex and explain it from a Christian perspective.

Did you tell them about the sacredness of their virginity? "Well, no, we can't do that, because it's unconstitutional." God says that when these laws were broken under the Old Covenant, the people were put to death. They were history. Under the New Testament, thank God for His grace and forgiveness.

Verses 28-30 of Deuteronomy, chapter 22, say:

> "If a man finds a young woman *who is* a virgin, who is not betrothed, and he seizes her and lies with her, and they are found out, then the man who lay with her shall give to the young woman's father fifty *shekels* of silver, and she shall be his wife because he has humbled her; he shall not be permitted to divorce her all his days.
>
> A man shall not take his father's wife, nor uncover his father's bed."

We need to acknowledge that the sacredness, the value, and the importance of sex was established by God, and we need to save our virginity until we can give it to the one person with whom we make a lifetime covenant.

If you have been married previously or you have been involved with a sexual partner or partners outside of the marriage covenant, you need to repent and get right with God. You need to live as a virgin until you dedicate yourself to one person and come into a lifetime blood covenant with that person. That's the perspective that we need to have as Christians.

Application of Family Covenant Truths

Please answer each of these statements/questions using Chapter 7 as your source of information:

1. Virginity under the Old Testament law meant: _____

   _____

   _____

   _____

2. A female, under Old Testament law, who had lost her virginity before marriage, faced _____

   _____ .

3. The Old Testament punishment for adultery, according to Deuteronomy 22:22, was _____ .

4. Sex is sacred to me because: _____

   _____

   _____

   _____

Sex in the Marriage Relationship

> Marriage *is* honorable among all, and the bed undefiled; but fornicators and adulterers God will judge.
> Hebrews 13:4

For the married man and woman, sex is a celebration of their covenant and life together. But outside of marriage, God says He is going to judge fornicators and adulterers.

Fornication is an all-encompassing term that has to do with pornography and sexual intercourse among homosexuals or lesbians as well as sexual activity outside of marriage. *Adultery* is a sexual relationship with someone who is married and someone they are not married to, whether the person is married or single.

Even though we are under the mercy and grace of God as New Testament believers, God still says that He is going to judge fornication and adultery, not in the same manner as He did in the Old Testament, because the judgment has changed. The principle, however, remains the same. God still sees adultery and fornication as sin, and He will judge it.

God still sees adultery and fornication as sin, and He will judge it.

Notice this statement, **The marriage bed is undefiled.** As Christians, we should have the most free, open, fun, fulfilling, and rewarding sex lives of anyone on earth.

The world comes across as being sexually free and fulfilled, while Christians are portrayed as uptight people who are afraid of sex. This is reversed as to how God says it is to be. God's plan is that there be an openness, a blessing on the marriage bed, and an enjoyment of one another. We should recognize that sex is not only a privilege, but it is a need in our lives. There should be no shame, no timidity, no avoidance or bad feelings toward sex.

I want to show you a biblical principle for a good sex life in the marriage. I don't want to be vulgar, but I want to be very plain so there will be no possibility of misunderstanding. Your sexual relationship is a primary part of the success of your marriage. It cannot be brushed off as something that's no big deal. On the other hand, it cannot be built up as something that is all-encompassing. It is a primary part of the success of your marriage, but it is not the only part. In the world, we build sex up to be at the center of everything.

Many times when a movie is advertised, sex is used to sell it, using a scene that has nothing to do with the plot of the movie. Sex is used in selling cigarettes, beer, and cars. In the world, sex is blown out of proportion and is exploited and overemphasized. It has been made dirty and carnal.

As Christians we don't agree with the world's exploitation of sex, yet in some Christian's minds, we have made sex unimportant, carnal, and worldly in the sense that we don't want to be involved with it. Some say, "It's no big deal. We have a good marriage regardless of what's going on in the marriage bed."

And some Christian women, because of past hurts and problems and fears, ignore the issue of sex and put it off as something that is not spiritual. As a result, they don't want to be involved with it. And there are Christian men who have done the same thing. Both of these ditches are wrong.

If you think you are to avoid sex because you are so spiritual, you are wrong. You are messing up your marriage relationship because of your perverted ideas of how the sexual relationship should be. By avoiding it and denying it, you are missing part of God's plan for your marriage. The husband and the wife should be emotionally and physically fulfilled through their sexual relationship. The sexual climax or orgasm is not only a gift, it is an enjoyable and needed part of the marriage relationship.

It is necessary to keep the emotional balance in the marriage right. When Christian couples are not enjoying a biblical sex life, there will be stresses and pressures that throw the emotional makeup off. It may be seen in your attitude at work or in other areas. There must be a biblical sexual release and a regular climax or orgasm for both the man and the woman, not only for the enjoyment, but also for the stability in their relationship.

Sex is not just for men. The fulfillment of the wife, as well as the husband, is very important. Some women deny, avoid, or push their husband away, and the lack of sexual fulfillment, the lack of climax on a regular basis, is hurting the husband and the marriage relationship. There must be this union, completion, and fulfillment of the celebration of the marriage covenant in a regular sexual relationship.

In Proverbs, chapter 5, starting with verse 15, we're going to see a description of the woman who helped the husband in meeting her needs.

> Drink water from your own cistern, and running water from your own well. Should your fountains be dispersed abroad, streams of water in the streets? Let them be only your own, and not for strangers with you. Let your fountain be blessed, and rejoice with the wife of your youth, as a loving deer and a graceful doe, let her breasts satisfy you at all times; and always be enraptured with her love. For why should you, my son, be enraptured with an immoral woman, and be embraced in the arms of a seductress? For the ways of man *are* before the eyes of the Lord, and He ponders all his paths.
>
> Proverbs 5:15-21

In this passage, the woman is described as a cistern and a well, the man as a fountain. The well is still or calm, and must be drawn out. You have to have a pump, a bucket, a cup, or something to draw out of a well, but you don't need anything to draw out of a fountain.

God is saying to the men, "Don't let your fountain be dispersed in the streets." In other words, don't have sex with an immoral woman, with a woman you pick up at some bar, with a woman on the corner, or with a woman who is married to someone else. But be enraptured with the wife of your youth. Be committed and involved sexually in a way that is intoxicating with the wife of your youth. That's what the word *enraptured* means in verse 19, **Let her breasts satisfy you at all times; and always be <u>enraptured</u>** [intoxicated] **<u>with her love</u>.**

Be committed and involved sexually in a way that is intoxicating with the wife of your youth.

Women are aroused sexually, mentally, and emotionally, but not physically. The well must be drawn out. So the wife must be stimulated mentally and emotionally before she is physically ready to be sexually active. Usually, men don't know that, so they are lying next to a well of live, fresh, pure, clear water, and we are mad because the well isn't jumping on us. But no well just jumps out! It must be drawn out, stimulated, and aroused. That starts mentally and emotionally.

Few men realize that having good sex at night starts with the way they talk to their wife in the morning. It starts with the way you kiss her good-bye. It starts with the way you act at the dinner table.

Yet, when we kiss the wife and children good-bye, we're in a hurry, and we're off to work. When we come home, our mind is full, we're tired, and we sit down at the table. The wife asks, "How is everything?" "Fine." "How was your day?" "Great." "What about such-and-such?" "It's fine." And the kids ask, "Dad, can you do this?" "No, I don't feel like it. Can't you just give me a little space?"

We sit and read the newspaper or watch the news. The wife asks, "How are you doing?" We respond, "Huh?" She asks, "You want some coffee?" "Okay." We've been sitting on our rusty dusty for a couple of hours, and now we're ready to go to bed. The wife has been fixing dinner, cleaning up, putting everything away, getting the kids bathed and off to bed, and now she finally sits down and the husband is ready for sex.

He thinks that just because he stands up, she is now excited. "Honey, I'm ready now," he says. She's supposed to cut a cartwheel and say, "Finally, my man has arisen!"

Not really! By this time she is done with you, because you have done nothing to draw out of her all day. When you left in the morning, you just left. You didn't leave her feeling loved, and when you got home, you didn't draw anything out of her. You simply went through your manly routine, so when you go to bed, she's not interested.

She may perform physically, but this is why most women have sex and don't climax. They go through the physical duty, but they are not drawn out as a well of water. They are not aroused and stimulated. They just do their duty. Husbands may never admit it, but they feel bad when the wife goes through the sexual act of intercourse but know she is not really fulfilled. Most husbands fail to do what it takes to draw out of that well so she can climax and be excited and fulfilled.

A good sexual relationship starts in the morning. The husband can do the dishes or load the dishwasher for his wife. That may be the most sexually arousing thing she's had in a long time! You have to stimulate your wife emotionally and mentally to remind her of why she wanted to be with you, why she likes you, and why she wanted to marry you. It wasn't because of your body, although some men are under the deceived notion that their macho image will help her climax and be sexually fulfilled.

Your macho image has nothing to do with your wife's sexual fulfillment. You're not a good sexual partner just because you have muscles, you are cool, or you wear bikini underwear. She doesn't care about your zebra-striped underwear! It may have worked in the movie, but the woman in the movie just had a part to read! That's not real life.

The bottom line issue in your wife's sexual fulfillment is how to "emotionally" draw out of that well. How to "emotionally" and "mentally" stimulate the relationship.

Now, as you move along in your sexual relationship, you go from the emotional part to the physical part. While a man starts with the physical and ends with the physical, the woman goes from the mental and the emotional into the physical. So her state of mind and her emotions must be right. The husband must be patient. The woman will probably need more time to come to sexual fulfillment than the man thinks she should take, but that's part of the relationship.

Make her fulfillment more important than your own. Give yourself to her fulfillment, no matter how long it takes. She will probably need manual stimulation and perhaps an artificial lubricant to help her in the physical process of the sexual relationship, but that's your job as a man to help her meet whatever need there is and to make sure that she is fulfilled.

If the husband is not sensitive to the wife's needs, usually she will back up sexually. She will go through the routine once a month or twice a month and do her duty, but she is never really excited about it. The husband becomes frustrated, because he wants his wife to be excited about sex and to give herself freely and totally to it. Often, the husband blames her, when in fact, he is the problem.

If the husband works in construction or heavy equipment, his hands may be calloused and rough, and he may smell like last week's dead dog! Don't expect your wife to be cuddly and warm and sexually excited if you are not sensitive to what it takes to draw out from her.

And never violate your spouse's conscience. The husband and wife need to talk and come into agreement and understanding of what is right for their sexual relationship. It may change through the years as you grow closer together, but if you violate your spouse's conscience, you may close her heart to you for a long time.

Go For God's Best!

I want to challenge and encourage both husbands and wives to go for *God's best* in the sexual aspect of your marriage relationship. Just like you want God's will in your prayer life and in every other aspect of your Christian walk, don't settle for less than His "best" in your sexual relationship with your spouse.

God made your body and designed it to be satisfied and fulfilled sexually. The husband may need some training and the wife may need to do some changing, but it will be worth it. Sexual fulfillment, romance, and intimacy are for both husband and wife, and the sexual climax or orgasm is a necessary part of the marriage for both people. Sex isn't just a "benefit," it's a necessary part of the marriage relationship.

Sexual fulfillment, romance, and intimacy are for both husband and wife.

I believe there is something spiritual as well as psychological that happens when a husband and wife come to a sexual climax regularly that causes them to stay one flesh. Something happens in their spirit and in their soul that keeps them one flesh.

If you are not experiencing sexual fulfillment, you are missing out on a necessary part of your marriage relationship. This is why so many marriages break up, even Christian marriages, because they don't have that sexual union that adds glue to the marriage. When God brought the man and woman together, He talked about "cleaving." The word *cleaving* has to do with being stuck together. They are to be stuck together in such a way that their soul and spirit are glued through the unity of their flesh.

The King James Version of Genesis 2:24 says, **Therefore shall a man leave his father and mother, and shall <u>cleave</u> unto his wife: and they shall be one flesh.** If you haven't been very good at cleaving, you need to make some changes.

Suggestions For Improving Your Sexual Relationship

Here are a few guidelines for making a good sexual relationship even better:

Communicate with each other as husband and wife to learn what is satisfying and what is not satisfying in your sexual relationship. Your wife is not going to like certain things that you think are really cool just because you saw so-and-so do it in a movie. Maybe she hasn't said anything because she doesn't want to hurt your feelings.

I used to say a particular word to Wendy that really aggravated her. When I read the pre-marriage counseling manual, that word wasn't in the book. I didn't even know why I said it, but I was trying to say things that would help and encourage and express my love for her. Finally she said, "Don't say that." "Okay, no way. I'll never say it again." But I didn't know how she felt until she told me, and we had been married for seventeen years at the time. You can be with someone for so long, yet keep learning about each other. This indicates a need to keep the communication going.

After you've had sexual intercourse and you've both been fulfilled, *remember to hold each other and talk to underscore your love and make it more than just a physical thing.* Sometimes the husband is off to the next deal — sleeping or whatever. It's so important to your sexual union to make it more than a physical activity, a real celebration of your covenant and love together.

Every time you have sex, it's probably not going to rate a "ten" (ten being highest on the scale). But just enjoy one another and make sure that you are regularly fulfilled.

The environment must be right for the celebration of your love. Sometimes the biggest hindrance to the sexual relationship is that the wife is not able to relax and participate because she is nervous about other things going on. Communicate and make your environment right. Learn what is the best time of day for each other. By the time you get together at night, if the wife works or is caring for children, she may be fatigued.

As I mentioned earlier, the woman's body responds differently than a man's body. The guy could be next to dead and still perform sexually. The guy could be a firefighter who just ran fifty-seven flights of stairs, put out fires on every floor all by himself, went back to his department, washed the truck, refilled the tank and got home totally wasted. "I've got to go to bed, honey," he announces. She asks, "You want to have sex?" "Okay!" He's rejuvenated and alive. He can handle it!

A woman who is emotionally and physically tired is not as responsive sexually. At the same time, wives, don't constantly look for an excuse to be tired. Sometimes "tired" is an attitude. I'm not trying to give excuses, but I'm trying to help us understand each other a little better.

Plan certain times to be extra special. Husbands, be aware that your wife is going to change at different times depending on what's going on with her physical and emotional clock, and wives, be aware that we can't read your mind. We love you, but we can't see inside you. We wish there was a little computer screen we could look at and it would say, "Do these five things." Since we don't have that, you have to tell us and help us.

Guys, shower, shave, and smell good!

If you have children, put a lock on your bedroom door. If you hear the kids coming, the husband says, "Get back in your beds," and he continues on, but the wife is finished. Emotionally, it doesn't work the same for her.

If you have a telephone in your bedroom, turn the phone off or use an answering machine. Again, if there is a phone interruption, the husband carries on but the wife is finished.

Remove all hindrances and make sex fun and fulfilling.

The "Right" and "Wrong" in a Sexual Relationship

> One person esteems *one* day above another; another esteems every day *alike*. Let each be fully convinced in his own mind. He who observes the day, observes *it* to the Lord; and he who does not observe the day, to the Lord he does not observe *it*. He who eats, eats to the Lord, for he gives God thanks; and he who does not eat, to the Lord he does not eat, and gives God thanks. For none of us lives to himself, and no one dies to himself. For if we live, we live to the Lord; and if we die, we die to the Lord. Therefore, whether we live or die, we are the Lord's.
>
> So then each of us shall give account of himself to God. Therefore let us not judge one another anymore, but rather resolve this, not to put a stumbling block or a cause to fall in *our* brother's way. I know and am convinced by the Lord Jesus that *there* is nothing unclean of itself; but to him who considers anything to be unclean, to him *it is* unclean.
>
> Romans 14:5-8,12-14

Something can be right to one person, but wrong for another. When we're talking about the sexual relationship, immediately we get a lot of personal opinions. We get a lot of things stirred up. The biblical way to resolve differences in your sexual desires is for the husband and wife to communicate until you come to a place of agreement. Both should be willing to give until they are in agreement.

Now, the sexual relationship between a husband and a wife does not have legalistic standards that say "this is good and that's not." Get into agreement, communicate, and share until both of you come to a place where you are satisfied sexually.

Husbands, we cannot force things on our wives, telling them we expect them to do things a certain way in bed. Some men want their wives to dress a certain way or dance around in the bedroom before they have sex. You're trying to get her to perform for you so you will be fulfilled. You're not giving, serving, and loving; you're lusting. *You are to give to her and serve her.* If you have her do something she is uncomfortable with, she won't be excited because you are violating her conscience.

On the other hand, there are some wives who connive, manipulate, and use sex as a tool to get what they want. In the process they are playing the role of a prostitute: "For a little bit of money, I'll give you my body." Maybe it's not money, but something she wants her husband to do.

Usually he will respond, "Okay, I'll play the game and get what I want." Now you've got a whore monger and a whore living in the same house — a whore monger and a whore who happen to be married, but who are operating outside of biblical principles and wondering why they're having such a hard time in their sex life. Both husband and wife are out of the Word. Both are selfish and focused on what they can get for themselves, and it's tearing the marriage apart. You've got to stop and get back to giving and communicating to determine, "What can we agree on that's right for our sexual relationship?"

Romans 14:5 says, **Let each be fully convinced in his own mind.** You've got to talk about what you think is right or wrong in the sexual relationship. How often should you have sex? First Corinthians 7 says the only time you should deprive one another is when you give yourself to fasting and prayer. If you use that as a guideline, not as a law, that would mean you should be having sex every one to three days. Once or twice a week would be a normal sex life.

In saying this I need to stress that this is a guideline. There are many factors that may cause the need for adjustments. There are travel and work schedules, a woman's monthly cycle, the adjustment of a new child, physical challenges in yourself or a family member, etc. So, when I say "normal" I mean in general. Sex every night is not reasonable, but more frequent sex during certain times, a vacation for example, is not unreasonable. Again, it is not meant to be law, and it should not be used as such. On the other hand, you cannot continually be looking for excuses not to have sex with your mate.

If you are depriving your husband, you are outside of the will of God and you are destroying your marriage. If you are depriving or avoiding your wife, you are destroying your marriage. You need a regular sex life. If you take a biblical perspective, you would want to have sex more often. Some spouses are still carrying hurts from their past and are taking it out on their mate in the sexual arena.

Recently, a frustrated husband came to me and said, "My wife won't give me a French kiss. She doesn't want her tongue in my mouth or my tongue in her mouth. She only kisses me like I'm her son, and I can only kiss her like she's my mother."

Maybe there is a physical challenge. If you only brush your teeth once every six months, or your mouth is an ash tray, I would say she has a right to put tape over your mouth. But if you're a clean person and you use mouthwash, she may be dealing with something that causes her to be hurt, closed, and resistant to any kind of intimacy in the sexual relationship.

You need to do some talking, because there is nothing unclean about French kissing. If you're closed, upset, or uptight about certain things, you need to talk them through together. You need to work it through so you and your spouse can relax and get into agreement.

The Bible doesn't tell you all the details of right or wrong. It does say in the Song of Solomon, however, that you should be kissing your wife's neck and her breasts.

The marriage bed is undefiled. As a husband and wife, communicate and come into harmony, and you can make your sex life fun and fulfilling. You can make it something you enjoy rather than something you struggle with.

Satan tries to bring division and perversion in the area of sex, which is a source of fighting, pain, and problems. But if you make sex good, it is a source of strength and unity and endorses the commitment you have to each other.

Application of Family Covenant Truths

Please answer each of these statements/questions using Chapter 8 as your source of information:

1. In the marriage relationship, sex is a celebration of:

_____

_____

_____

2. "The marriage bed is undefiled" means: _____

_____

_____

_____

3. Sex in marriage is important because: _____

_____

_____

_____

4. I will go for "God's best" in my sexual relationship in marriage by:

_____

_____

_____

_____

5. To "cleave" together as husband and wife means:

_____

_____

_____

6. Four ways to make my sexual relationship with my spouse fun and fulfilling are:

a. _____
_____

b. _____
_____

c. _____
_____

d. _____
_____

"Giving" and "Serving" One Another

I n I Corinthians, chapter 7, Paul is addressing the Corinthians who came from a heathen background. Corinth was a corrupt city, full of idolatry. They worshipped false gods through sex, so they were active in bisexuality, homosexuality, lesbianism, and all kinds of sexual perversion.

Corinth had over a thousand prostitutes in one temple where the men went to supposedly worship these false gods by having illicit sex with the prostitutes. Corinth was what we might call "the ghetto of the ghetto" in terms of sexual immorality.

So Paul says to the city of Corinth in verse 1 of chapter 7: **It is good for a man not to touch a woman.** In other words, just stay single until you get your mind renewed and your life right. Then you can have the kind of marriage that God wants you to have. You need a little time to let the Holy Ghost and the Word of God sanctify your life from the dirt of the past. This is true today as well.

In the matter of divorce and remarriage, people tend to jump right into more problems before getting some things cleaned out of their lives. Some are dating and they're not even divorced.

Paul was saying, it would be better for you not to touch a woman and give yourself time to get your life cleaned up. Paul is not contradicting God's Word, "I want you to be married and have a partner for life, because it's not good for you to be alone." But he is saying, "Because of the immorality of your past, give yourself some time to get cleaned up before you dive into another relationship. Catch your breath!"

Many people are divorced the second time, the third time, or the fourth time, and on and on, because they have never changed the problems of their first marriage. They kept diving into a new relationship. Some people pick up boyfriends and girlfriends quicker than I could pick up groceries at the store. When Paul said, *It is* **good for a man not to touch a woman**, he was saying, "Don't dive into a new relationship until you have recovered, have made some changes, and are healed and sanctified."

Don't dive into a new relationship until you have recovered, have made some changes, and are healed and sanctified.

If I say something that steps on your toes, please don't feel condemned. My goal is for you to know the truth, because the truth will make you free (John 8:32). Most of the things I am discussing, I have to deal with myself. I haven't been divorced, but truth confronts all of us. We are seeking to change, not to be condemned, or react and get mad. Let's be the kind of people who say, "Lord, if it's in the Book, I'm going to go for it. I'm not going to resist it and react to it."

> Nevertheless, because of sexual immorality, let each man have his own wife, and let each woman have her own husband.
>
> I Corinthians 7:2

Paul is saying, "Look, I know you aren't going to be able to stay single very long, because you're going to start desiring to have sexual relationships since you've been so involved with it in the world. So find a wife (or a husband), and let that person be your only sexual partner. Don't have other people's wives or husbands, or 'spare' people floating in between!"

> Let the husband render to his wife the affection due her, and likewise also the wife to her husband. The wife does not have authority over her own body, but the husband *does*. And likewise the husband does not have authority over his own body, but the wife *does*. Do not deprive one another except with consent for a time, that you may give yourselves to fasting and prayer; and come together again so that Satan does not tempt you because of your lack of self-control.
>
> I Corinthians 7:3-5

What Paul is saying is, "You should have your own spouse and a regular sexual relationship." The only time you stop your regular sexual relationship is when you are in agreement to do so for the purpose of fasting and prayer. The point I'm trying to make is that you do not have power over your own body. You don't have authority over your own body, because you're not in the sexual relationship for what you can get for yourself. *You're in it for what you can give to your spouse.*

You're in the sexual relationship for what you can give to your spouse.

Generally, women are better givers than men. How many times have you heard a man say, "I really want to tithe, but my wife won't let me"? I rarely hear that. But I have had dozens of women say, "I want to tithe, but my husband won't let me." Why? Because men are generally selfish.

Women are quicker to serve. They'll get up from the table and pick up the dishes while the man sits there. You've been eating for forty-seven years, using dishes and silverware all the time, and you still haven't thought about picking up a plate! Why? Because you're retarded? No, you're a man! Now, many of us saved Christian men are givers and helpers. But generally, men are more selfish.

The heart of the average man is selfish when it comes to sex. He may love his wife and really care and he may be a committed Christian, but when it comes to sex, his natural inclination is getting, not giving. That's why the average man will climax and feel sexually satisfied while his wife feels empty, and he just doesn't get it. He's thinking about himself, not her.

Paul said, **The wife does not have authority over her own body, but the husband does, and likewise the husband does not have authority over his own body, but the wife does** (I Corinthians 7:4).

I do not have power over my own body, my wife does. She does not have power over her own body, but I do. I want to meet her needs and use my authority and influence over her body to fulfill and satisfy her. The biblical principle is, when you give, it will be given unto you. *You will get more if you give more.*

Some men would be quick to say, "Well, my wife just doesn't want to have sex very much." I guarantee you, at least one part of the reason is because you are thinking about you, not her, and she's tired of it. Greed and selfishness will tear down the marriage relationship.

When you get two immature people in a marriage relationship and both are trying to get something from each other, no one is giving and both are taking, the marriage will crumble quickly. But when you get mature people, with both giving into the marriage and fulfilling one another, the more you give, the more you will receive. But both have to give.

The basis of all marriage fighting is, "You should do this for me. You should change this." Selfishness! But if we could get into a giving mode, where we're trying to outgive each other, I guarantee you, there would be more enjoyment and fulfillment.

As a husband, your focus should be, "How can I fulfill my wife sexually? How can I make it so good that she is excited about our one-flesh relationship?" That should be foremost in your mind when you are having sex with your mate.

Application of Family Covenant Truths

Please answer each of these statements/questions using Chapter 9 as your source of information:

1. To be sanctified from my past means: _____

   _____

   _____

   _____

2. A time for recovery and healing will: _____

   _____

   _____

   _____

3. The only reason for a husband and wife to deprive each other of sexual activity is: _____

   _____

   _____

4. I can improve our marital sexual relationship by:

   _____

   _____

   _____

   _____

Sex Outside the Marriage Relationship

Sex outside of the marriage union will never produce good results. Although there is pleasure in sin for a season, sex outside of the marriage relationship will be short-lived, but the pain will be long-lived.

Proverbs 6:23-25 gets right to the heart of immoral sexual relationships:

> For the commandment [God's Word] is a lamp, and the law a light; reproofs of instruction are the way of life, to keep you from the evil woman, from the flattering tongue of a seductress. Do not lust after her beauty in your heart.

God is against adultery, fornication, rape, and misuse of the sexual relationship in any way, because it always results in destruction for both people involved.

Every affair, every act of fornication or adultery, starts out with a man and a woman being friends and getting emotionally involved with each other:

- "I can talk to him better than I can talk to my own husband."
- "I talk to her more than I talk to my own wife."
- "I feel something there that I've never felt before."

All of these are words that have been spoken to me by people entering a sexual relationship with someone other than their marriage partner.

Sex outside of the marriage relationship will be short-lived, but the pain will be long-lived.

Any man who begins to feel emotionally involved with a woman is on his way to adultery or fornication unless he breaks that relationship off. And don't think it will never happen to you. The guy who says, "It will never happen to me," is deceived.

Proverbs 6:25,26 says:

> Do not lust after her beauty in your heart, nor let her allure you with her eyelids. For by means of a harlot *a man is reduced* to a crust of bread.

The "crust" is the part of bread you cut off and throw away. A mighty man starts to become a crust of bread when he looks at her eyelashes!

You may be saying, "I'm serving God. Nothing is going to happen to me." Yet, verses 26 and 27 say:

> For by means of a harlot *a man is reduced* to a crust of bread; and an adulteress will prey upon his precious life. Can a man take fire to his bosom, and his clothes not be burned?

You would think people would wise up and figure out that adultery and fornication do not produce good results. Yet, people keep getting ensnared in both of these areas.

> Can one walk on hot coals, and his feet not be seared? So *is* he who goes in to his neighbor's wife; whoever touches her shall not be innocent.
>
> Proverbs 6:28,29

You can't say, "I couldn't help it. I didn't mean to. I'm innocent. It wasn't my fault." You are *not* innocent when you find yourself in adultery.

We've got to stay clean and pure and keep our sexual gift right to make it a blessing and not a curse. To the married man and woman, sex is a celebration of their love and their covenant together.

To the married man and woman, sex is a celebration of their love and their covenant together.

> For at the window of my house I looked through my lattice, and saw among the simple, I perceived

109

among the youths, a young man devoid of understanding, passing along the street near her corner; and he took the path to her house.

Proverbs 7:6-8

Now, the problem starts when you hang around her corner. Young folks, if you are out with somebody of the opposite sex and you park your car where no one else is and you start stroking each other, you're going to ignite a fire. It doesn't matter if you're in love. It doesn't matter if God wants you together. It doesn't matter if you're saved or unsaved, Spirit-filled or not. You start touching each other and you're going to have a fire. So don't go by that corner!

Don't park your car and hang out, and make out. Don't go into a single man or single woman's apartment and sit on the couch next to each other to watch TV, because your mind isn't on TV. You hang around the corner, and the door will open for problems to come. So, as a single person, don't put yourself in that position. Even if you don't do anything, it's not scriptural to go into a single's apartment alone. The Bible says, **Abstain from all appearance of evil** (1 Thessalonians 5:22 KJV).

Two single people hanging out in an apartment make it appear like something is happening. But you say, "We're Christians. We have a fish on our car bumpers." What's on your bumper won't stop you from igniting each other's flesh!

In Proverbs 7, the young man was hanging around and he took the path to the house of the seductress. If he wouldn't have gone to her house, the whole thing wouldn't have started.

In the twilight, in the evening, in the black and dark night.

And there a woman met him, *with* the attire of a harlot, and a crafty heart.

> She *was* loud and rebellious, her feet would not
> stay at home.
> At times *she* was outside, at times in the open
> square, lurking at every corner.
> So she caught him and kissed him; with an impu-
> dent face she said to him:
> I *have* peace offerings with me.
>
> Proverbs 7:9-14

Spiritualizing adultery will not make it good. Putting "Christianese" on your fornication does not make it blessed by God. I know of a single couple who got a bottle of wine and some crackers and had communion. Now, I was born at night but not last night! They were going to have communion, and it was just a "coincidence" that they ended up having sex! They didn't mean to do that, of course, but they really wanted to be spiritual. Come on, you can't spiritualize the lust of your flesh.

Spiritualizing adultery will not make it good.

Another case in point: For a married person to be in love with someone you're not married to, or to "lust" for someone you're not married to, and then say the Lord brought you together, is a lie. You are shaming the Lord, the One you say you love. You are embarrassing the God you say you serve. To blame God for the lust of your flesh, for adultery or fornication, or even the desire for it, makes it doubly bad. If you are going to sin, just say, "I want to sin," but don't pull God in on it.

That's like a couple who came to our altar and asked me to pray for their marriage. I said, "Oh, you are getting married?" They said, "Yes, as soon as the divorces are final." I said, "What?" "Well, we're both married to someone else, but we found out we married the wrong people. God brought us together, and He told us we're supposed to be married as soon as the divorces are final."

I said, "I can't pray for you. How am I going to get God's blessing on your sins?" They were offended. They said, "You don't love us and you're judging us." I said, "I don't have to judge you, the Bible already did."

If you are in sin and someone says, "Sister [or brother], come on, that isn't right," and you take their response as judgment, realize that the judgment is not of a man, it's of God. They're only saying it because they love you and are trying to spare your soul from hell.

Like Proverbs 6:27 says, you can't take fire into your bosom without getting burned. When people do get burned, then they say, "Pray for me. I'm hurt." Then we pray with them, but wouldn't it have been better if they would have received godly counsel *before* they got burned?

The seductress in Proverbs 7 goes on: **So I came out to meet you, diligently to seek your face, and I have found you** (v. 15). Can't you just hear it? "You're the one I've been looking for. My husband is not like you. He doesn't talk to me the way you do." Or, "My wife isn't like you. She doesn't understand me like you do. I've been looking for someone like you. Oh, you're the one. It's obvious to me that I missed God, but now I've found God's will."

> "I have spread my bed with tapestry, colored coverings of Egyptian linen. I have perfumed my bed with myrrh, aloes, and cinnamon. Come, let us take our fill

of love until morning; let us delight ourselves with love. For my husband *is* not at home; he has gone on a long journey; he has taken a bag of money with him, *and* will come home on the appointed day."

With her enticing speech she caused him to yield, with her flattering lips she seduced him. Immediately he went after her, as an ox goes to slaughter, or as a fool to the correction of the stocks, till an arrow struck his liver. As a bird hastens to the snare, he did not know it *would* cost his life.

Proverbs 7:16-23

That doesn't mean you'll be dead physically or spiritually, but your life will never be the same. You will lose a part of your life. Let's not give our lives up for some fleeting physical satisfaction. Let's keep our hearts and actions right so we can have God's blessing in every part of our lives.

Application of Family Covenant Truths

Please answer each of these statements/questions, using Chapter 10 as your source of information:

1. An emotional relationship with a person of the opposite sex usually results in: _____
   _____
   _____

2. The best way I can avoid sexual temptation is: _____
   _____
   _____
   _____

3. To receive godly counsel I: _____
   _____
   _____
   _____

4. The end result of seduction is: _____
   _____
   _____

Keeping Life in Your Marriage Relationship

> *He* who finds a wife finds a good *thing*, and obtains favor from the Lord.
>
> Proverbs 18:22

Esteeming One Another

Husbands and wives, you can keep life in your marriage relationship by treating your spouse as a gift from God, as a "valued treasure."

Proverbs 12:4 says, **An excellent wife *is* the crown of her husband, but she who causes shame *is* like rottenness in his bones.** Wives, value your husband and be the crown in his life. Husbands, see your wife as that valuable crown to your life who gives you more meaning and glory.

Proverbs 19:14 says, **Houses and riches *are* an inheritance from fathers, but a prudent wife *is* from the Lord.** In other words, anybody can get houses and riches, but you need God's help to find a prudent wife.

How would you treat your spouse if you really believed they were a gift from God?

One man came to me and said, "I don't know if I can make it. I left my wife and now I want her back." As we talked and prayed, he said, "Now I know how much I want her as my wife." Sometimes we are so foolish that we lose our gift before we realize it was a gift. Value your spouse and keep your marriage alive by realizing God gave this man (or woman) to you.

Maybe God gave you a shiny trophy and you have tarnished it. Or maybe you are tarnishing each other. Begin to value your spouse again, and life and glory will come back into your relationship.

Family — High on the Priorities List

Another thing you can do to keep life in your marriage relationship is to *make your family more important than anything, other than Jesus.* We should be willing to sacrifice anything, other than our relationship with the Lord, for our family. Many will sacrifice their family for their job, packing up and moving to a place they don't want to be just to have a job. My family is more important to me than a job.

Make your family more important than anything, other than Jesus.

God does not judge you based on what job you have. But He does judge you based on how you raise your family. So make sure you never get the two reversed, sacrificing your family just to keep a job.

If your job is costing you a relationship with your kids, tell your boss that you have two choices: Either to change or adjust the hours you work in that company, or to leave because your family is more important to you. Money is meaningless if your little boy becomes a drunk, or your wife sleeps with your neighbor because you are working all the time.

God will favor your life and honor your faithfulness to value your wife and kids.

Men, is your family more important to you than your golf buddies or your bowling buddies? Many husbands are up early to go to their clubs or to be on the course by 7:30 a.m. for a tee time. Because you never get that excited to get up and have a cup of coffee with your wife, she may be jealous of your buddies. By your actions, you are saying that they are more important to you than your wife.

When you go to games, take your wife with you and sit and eat popcorn with her. Or take her to the club and have coffee, lunch, or dinner together. Your family should be more important to you than anyone else. Guard, protect, and value them.

Primary Needs

Paul offers godly counsel for husband-wife relationships in Ephesians, chapter 5, verses 22-33:

> Wives, submit to your own husbands, as to the Lord. For the husband is head of the wife, as also Christ is head of the church; and He is the Savior of the body.
>
> Therefore, just as the church is subject to Christ, so *let* the wives *be* to their own husbands in everything.
>
> Husbands, love your wives, just as Christ also loved the church and gave Himself for her, that He might sanctify and cleanse her with the washing of water by the word, that He might present her to Himself a glorious church, not having spot or wrinkle or any such thing, but that she should be holy and without blemish.

So husbands ought to love their own wives as their own bodies; he who loves his wife loves himself. For no one ever hated his own flesh, but nourishes and cherishes it, just as the Lord *does* the church. For we are members of His body, of His flesh and of His bones.

"For this reason a man shall leave his father and mother and be joined to his wife, and the two shall become one flesh."

This is a great mystery, but I speak concerning Christ and the church. Nevertheless let each one of you in particular so love his own wife as himself, and let the wife *see* that she respects *her* husband.

In this Scripture passage, two primary needs of the marriage relationship are identified:

1. **Husbands, love your wives** (v. 25), and

2. **Wives, submit to your own husbands, as to the Lord** (v. 22).

Husbands, love your wife. Don't abuse her. Don't misuse her. Don't assume or take her for granted. Love your wife just as Jesus loved the Church. He was willing to give everything for the Church — to lay down His life for the Church.

Often we say, "I'm doing everything for my wife and for my family," when in fact, we're not. Much of what we are doing is for ourselves. The man who runs off to work every day and spends fourteen or fifteen hours at the office six and seven days a week, is not doing that for his wife. He is not doing it for his kids. That's the excuse he gives so he can look good and justify his behavior. In such a case, the husband is chasing the buck, chasing the corporate position, and living for his ego and his wallet. If you love your wife and kids and want to keep life in your marriage and family relationships, you will want to be with them, spend time with them, and do things with them.

Wives, submit to your husbands. This does not mean that you are to be a rug that he walks on or to go along with everything, and be barefoot, pregnant, and in the kitchen all the time. That didn't come from the Bible. The Bible teaches that women should be businesswomen who have a staff and servants, and they are aggressive and leaders in many ways.

Submitting to your husband means that you recognize that he's the quarterback on the team — he's not the whole team. And when the quarterback calls the play, you don't argue over it. You just run the play. If the play doesn't work, he takes the heat.

In a real football game, can you imagine the quarterback calling the play and the other players saying, "We're tired of running that play"? The halfback and the end throw in their opinions. No, when the quarterback calls the play, you get in position. You run straight up the middle, you get knocked down for a loss. You get back in the huddle, and again, it's still up to the quarterback to call the play.

This is not the time for everybody to say, "I can't believe it, man. Your salary is three times my salary and you're calling dumb plays." You're going to get a penalty for delaying the game, or you're going to have confusion on the field because everybody is trying to do what they think is the right thing to do.

And so it goes in many homes today. We're fighting and squabbling over what play to call, and usually we end up being penalized for delaying the game because we're getting nowhere and doing nothing but fighting with each other.

Wives, submit to your husband and respect him. There will be areas where you will be wiser and smarter than he is. That's why God brought you together, so you would make up for his weaknesses and for him to make up for yours.

Let's say the wife is better when it comes to financial management, but the husband calls the plays. He says, "Here's what we are going to do with our money." He controls the checkbook and pays the bills, and pretty soon you find that you're behind, struggling, and in a financial crisis.

Now the wife steps in and begins to squabble and fight with her husband: "I can run this better than you. I can't believe how out of it you are. You're going to run us into the poorhouse. Had you not bought that dumb bicycle we wouldn't be in this mess. If you hadn't bought that boat and spent money on your bowling league, we wouldn't be in this situation."

Now you've got all of this stuff stirred up. You may be correct in your analysis and in your ability to solve the problem, but God can't work in your home now because it's full of strife and division.

Your husband isn't going to be able to see and hear because he's fighting you instead of fighting the problem. If you'll submit to your husband, one day with the help of God, he will say, "I am not good at managing the money. Honey, could you help?" And you're going to say, "I think I can manage it." The Lord will work where there is harmony and unity. The quarterback is still calling the shots, but the play he's calling gives you the ball in that area.

Husbands, when there is a problem in the home, ask yourself, "Am I really loving my wife?" Usually you will find that you have backslidden in that area. When there are problems and difficulties, the husband usually has his focus on other issues and he's not really loving and taking care of his wife.

Wives, when strife and problems are going on, ask yourself, "Am I really submitting to my husband, or am I competing with my husband?" In the process of loving and submitting, the number one key is *communication*.

Another way to keep your marriage alive is to *keep it fun and spiritual*. As a family, you can read the Word, pray, talk about the Lord, and discuss the things of God, sing, shout and praise the Lord together. Spirituality is a normal part of our home. I talk with my kids about the things of the Lord.

When Caleb was younger, I talked with him about boys and girls. He wrestled with the boys and they hit each other. Then he said he wrestled with the girls and they hit each other. I said, "Caleb, you can't hit the girls." "Why not?" Then we talked about the relationship between girls and boys.

I asked him if he felt anything different when he was around the girls. "Well, Dad, whenever you start talking about this stuff, I just want to go somewhere else." And I said, "Whenever I think about talking about this stuff, I want to go somewhere else, too, but we've got to talk." Even though you may be uncomfortable and don't know exactly what to say, talk and keep it spiritual.

We have three children and three Mariner baseball bats. One night when Micah was three years old, he hit his big brother Caleb in the head with his bat. While Caleb thought he was going to die, and we had a few similar thoughts, Micah was laughing. So I asked Micah, "Was that your bat that just connected with Caleb's head?" "Yes."

Typically as a parent, you would say, "Well, I buy you something nice and all you can do is beat each other up. I told you this was going to happen." But there are other options. Quickly I mustered all the spirituality I could and said, "Micah, come over here and pray for your brother and ask God to heal him." If you've ever seen a three year old laying hands on his seven-year-old brother and praying, you have seen a precious moment.

Keeping Your Sex Life Fulfilling and Fun

Another way to keep your marriage relationship alive is *to keep your sex life fulfilling and fun.*

Good sex is about married people who know each other better than anyone else knows them, enjoying their relationship well into their later years.

Good sex is about married people who know each other better than anyone else knows them, enjoying their relationship well into their later years.

In the case of some couples, when you first got together, you were sexy, romantic, and exciting. Then on the marriage day, something happened. You've been pecking each other ever since, and you don't even kiss good anymore. When you were dating you could sit in the car and kiss on each other for an hour and a half. Now you can't do anything for an hour and a half. Bitterness, resentment, and anger show up in a dead sex life.

Wendy and I met each other in Bible school and we talked a few times in class. We made plans to date and started building a relationship before and after classes at Bible school long before we ever dated. I was in a drug rehab center and I could only date once a month. And in Bible school, we could only date on Saturdays. But our first kiss was at the steps of her room at the Bible school dormitory. I remember it clearly.

After our first date, we had our first kiss, and she said, "Ooooh, you are a wet kisser." Recently, I said to her, "My kisses have been getting wetter ever since."

Some Christians think it's not spiritual to be romantic and sexually alive and it drains the life out of your marriage. Remember, Abraham was ninety-nine when Sarah was buying those little pregnancy tests every month!

Communicate

Another way to keep your marriage alive is to *practice the art of communication*. Again, Paul gives us some guidelines for the area of communication in Ephesians 4:29-32. Let's look at these verses:

> Let no corrupt word proceed out of your mouth, but what is good for necessary edification, that it may impart grace to the hearers. And do not grieve the Holy Spirit of God, by whom you were sealed for the day of redemption. Let all bitterness, wrath, anger, clamor, and evil speaking be put away from you, with all malice. And be kind to one another, tenderhearted, forgiving one another, even as God in Christ forgave you.

Few people are naturally good at communicating. That's why we must "practice" communicating. Young people particularly have a hard time expressing what they feel, and many people never grow out of that challenge. *All* of us need to practice the art of communication.

Here is an illustration of "practicing" communication. When you go to a doctor, you are going to his practice. He gets out of school and opens a practice. Why? Because he really doesn't know how to get you healed, but he is going to practice. He knows some things, but many times he is not sure, so he has a "practice." He wants you to come, not because he is an expert in everything, but because he wants to practice on you.

You need to have that attitude with your spouse in communicating. Sit down with him or her and "practice" communicating, sharing some of the things that you think and feel. Some days it will be good and some days it won't be so good, but keep practicing and you both will become better at it. In the next chapter, we will talk more in depth about developing your communication skills.

Application of Family Covenant Truths

Please answer each of these statements/questions using Chapter 11 as your source of information:

1. I treat my spouse as a gift from God by: _____

   _____

   _____

   _____

2. Some of the things I can do to keep life in my marriage relationship are: _____

   _____

   _____

   _____

   _____

3. The two primary needs of the marriage relationship are:

   a. _____
   b. _____

4. A marriage relationship is described in Ephesians 5 as Christ loving the Church. In light of this description, my marriage relationship should be: _____

   _____

   _____

   _____

   _____

5. To submit to a husband means: _____

_____

_____

_____

6. To keep my marriage and home free of strife and division, I will: _____

_____

_____

_____

_____

_____

7. I can help to improve communication in my marriage by: _____

_____

_____

_____

_____

_____

Developing Your Communication Skills

Communication is the foundation of the marriage relationship. Every problem we have in one way or another comes right back to a breakdown in communication.

If you have sexual problems, you can solve them with communication. If you have financial problems, usually there is a communication breakdown. You aren't getting into agreement and managing your resources properly, which results in struggling, anger, and fighting. If you have parent/child problems, usually the kids are using Dad against Mom, or Mom against Dad. Dad says, "Fine." Mom says, "I just told them not to do that." What's going on? A lack of communication. In one way or another, all of our problems go back to *communication issues*.

It is hard to have quality communication in the home. The person who says, "We never have a problem with communication," is the one who really scares me. The last person who told me, "We've never had a fight in our marriage," is divorced today. I'm serious about this. If you think that communication is just a natural, easy thing that happens automatically, you're out of touch with reality. Communication in the home is not just a natural happenstance. It must be practiced and developed, and it takes effort from both parties.

In some marriages, you talk *about* each other more than you talk *to* each other. You really have a breakdown in communication. If you are having communication challenges, don't feel that your marriage is doomed. If you will practice and work and apply yourself, you can improve.

When God brings two different people together, not only are they male and female, which makes them very different, but they are different in personality. Often, their backgrounds are different. Some have racial, age, or cultural differences. God brings them together and says, "Learn to get along, help each other, and be one."

Wendy doesn't think like I do, feel like I do, or do anything like I do, but even if she did, there would still be a challenge. I don't like myself sometimes, so how am I going to like her? She has her own perspective and thoughts. We are practicing and developing our communication skills. And although we have been working on it for over twenty years now, we're still learning and improving every day.

If you get real honest with yourself, half the things you say you believe, you're not sure. Half the fights you get in, you could take either side, it just depends on what day of the week it is. One day you say to your spouse, "We need to be kind and gentle with the kids." The next day you're saying, "We need to get a little discipline around this house." We all have so many different thoughts and feelings that it is difficult to flow in unity.

Ephesians, chapter 4, verse 29 KJV says, **Let no corrupt communication proceed out of your mouth.** For some of our homes, that means there wouldn't be a word spoken for probably the next month or two. I mean, if you stopped the corrupt communication and the negative, sarcastic talk, some of us wouldn't have anything to say.

> **Let no corrupt communication proceed out of your mouth, but that which is good to the use of edifying** [in other words, building up and encouraging], **that it may minister grace unto the hearers.**
> [*Grace* is God's blessing, His favor, and His Spirit. Impart His favor, blessing, and Spirit to people.]
> **And grieve not the Holy Spirit of God, whereby ye are sealed unto the day of redemption.**
> **Ephesians 4:30 KJV**

When we are squabbling, arguing, and going on and on in our sarcastic reaction towards each other, we are grieving the Holy Spirit. When He is grieved, He won't work.

If you're upset with your kids, saying things you don't really mean, your frustration is being expressed in your words, you are grieving the Holy Spirit. While the Holy Spirit is trying to bless your marriage and your children, you are grieving Him and driving Him out of your house. You are praying for your husband to be saved, then you say things that grieve the Holy Spirit so He can't work in your husband's life.

> **Let all bitterness, and wrath, and anger, and clamour, and evil speaking, be put away from you, with all malice: and be ye kind one to another, tenderhearted, forgiving one another, even as God for Christ's sake hath forgiven you.**
> **Ephesians 4:31,32 KJV**

129

And be ye kind one to another, tenderhearted, forgiving one another (Ephesians 4:32 KJV).

That's a mouthful of challenge when it comes to communication in the home! It is difficult because we are so quick to react to things that the spouse or the kids say, and many times the children will push you to the limit. You're frustrated so you say, "Can't you kids just do what you're told?" The kids are looking at you thinking, "Okay, does that mean I try once more, or should I do what I'm told right now?"

When you're in this kind of conflict, it's so easy to speak negatively: "I get so sick and tired of you kids. You're driving me crazy." Your own corrupt communication is stopping the grace of God from working in your family.

Because of the number of people who have gone through divorce or a marriage separation, even in our own church, they know what a communication breakdown means. So we've got to take these verses to heart and get real serious about the way we communicate with each other.

In verse 26 of Ephesians, chapter 4, Paul gives us some insight that will help us in our communication: *"Be angry, and do not sin"*: **do not let the sun go down on your wrath.**

God knows that we're going to get angry at times, and He is saying, "Just don't let your anger turn into sin." So how do we know the difference? For one thing, you carry your anger from day to day if it has turned into sin. It's okay to get angry, but it's not okay to let that anger affect your relationships and carry it on day after day. Usually when we get angry over little things, it's because we're carrying anger over big things. We keep it inside us day after day. The cat you kicked wasn't the problem. It's the stuff you are carrying inside day after day, not having released it through forgiveness.

The Lord created us, He made our emotions, and He understands that we're going to get angry. Does God ever get angry? The Bible mentions "the wrath of God" and "the anger of the Lord" several times. God gets angry, but He doesn't let it become sin.

There is no way around anger and frustration at times, but we're not to let it become sin. The key is to communicate about the things we are mad about instead of holding it inside and carrying it. If we will communicate, we'll not let the sun go down on our wrath.

We should take this verse very literally. Run to your spouse and say, "It's almost dark, honey, we've got to talk." Or, "Honey, before we go to bed, I've got to talk to you. I cannot take this anger to bed with me." Remember, what you take to bed with you that is negative, you will wake up with, except by morning it will be worse! The tension of the moment may be gone, but it's still sitting in your belly and rotting.

Garbage that you don't take out doesn't go away. It's still sitting in your kitchen, only it's rotting. Likewise, the garbage that you go to bed with just begins to rot in your belly. That's where ulcers, tumors, headaches and migraines, and frustrations and bitterness come from — anger that didn't get dealt with before the sun went down.

People will do things that make us mad. It could be big things or insignificant things. But anger is not the problem. It's *what we do with it* that can become the problem.

___

Anger is not the problem. It's what we do with it that can become the problem.

___

131

You're going to have days of excitement and enjoyment, and you're going to have days of frustration and anger. *How* you communicate about it is going to decide whether you are successful or not. It's not whether you go through things, it's *how* you go through them.

Just because you get angry with your spouse does not mean you have a bad marriage. The Bible says, "Be angry, just don't let it go into sin, where you begin to be controlled by it."

If you're married to a man, there will be times when you get angry. If you're married to a woman and you have kids, there are times you will be frustrated. Don't tell me you were happy when your kids colored your walls! Or you were excited when they threw eggs behind the washing machine! There will be times when you are frustrated, but just don't let the anger and frustration control you. Communicating is the key to dealing with it.

Five Keys to More Effective Communication

Here are five keys for developing successful communication skills. There may be other ways, too, but these are the primary ways.

1. **Don't give up, don't leave, and don't stop talking.**

This may be harder for men than for women, but I know some women who get silent, too. Just hang in there and keep talking. When you are silent, that's when things begin to boil and the pressure cooker builds. That's when assumptions are made.

Wendy and I have had to work on this, and we still do because of my tendency when things aren't going good to just be silent and go on about my business. Her response to my quietness is, "Fine."

Now, we've not only got the problem of not talking, we've got the added problem of who is going to humble himself first and break the silence. My thought is, "She knows I'm upset about this, and when she wants to get it straight, she'll come to me about it." I'm assuming her thought is, "He's supposed to be the one who is leading his family, and if he's going to be the man of this house, then he'll come to me and get it straight."

If you are walking around the house quiet, uptight, or not talking, you are letting the enemy get a foothold in your home. Ephesians 4:27 says, **Nor give place to the devil.** Without communicating, you are opening the door of your house to the devil.

Don't stop talking and don't leave. When you slam the door and walk out of the room, you have sown a seed for divorce. You separate yourself and that's a seed for divorce. When you leave one another, at first it's just for a few moments, for an evening, or for a day. "I'll be back. I need some time to think." Wham! Out the door you go. Every time you leave, you are getting better at it. You are sowing seeds for divorce. If you've planted this kind of seed and the harvest is coming up, get it changed quickly if you want to save your marriage.

When one spouse falls in a hole, don't jump in with them. It's easy to jump right in the same problem with your wife or your husband. When one spouse is mad and says, "I'm not going to talk about it," the other one needs to say, "Honey, let's keep talking." "I don't want to talk. You don't listen anyway." "Well, I'm really trying to listen. What were you saying?"

"Well, it makes me mad that you spent money again." "Yeah, I understand. I know you don't think it's right, but here is my perspective." "You've always got your perspective." "You're right, I do. What's your perspective?" "Here is what I think." "Yes, I can see why you think that, but I really wanted to...." "Well, maybe you shouldn't do what you really want to do." "You're right."

See, if you will just stay with it and keep talking, pretty soon you will meet in the middle of the road and say, "You're not so bad after all." But if both of you go quiet, it could go on for days. Somebody has to stay out of the hole and keep talking, although it's not always easy. But as you learn to come into agreement with each other, your marriage will grow stronger.

2. **Don't use your spouse's faults as a comeback or as an excuse for your faults.**

When you've been with a person for any length of time, you know their faults, and part of the problem we have in marriage is, we think about each other's faults more than we do about each other's strengths, and we need to change that. If you use what you know about each other as an excuse, you'll both spend the rest of your life excusing yourself rather than growing the kind of marriage and family that God wants you to have.

Your wife says, "Honey, you just let the kids do whatever they feel...you're just lazy. You should get up and discipline them." She's all upset, so your response is, "Well, let me tell you something about what I've been doing all week long while you sat around. I could handle this place in fifteen minutes while you talk about all the problems you've got."

You go on with your accusations about her faults rather than acknowledging what she was confronting in your faults. Both of you are probably right. The thing I want you to see is, it doesn't help either one of you to avoid the truth by accusing the other person.

It would be like Wendy confronting me because I didn't wash the car, and then I say to her, "You forgot to pick up the beans." What does that have to do with washing the car? Nothing! But it's my way of coming back and avoiding the issues by putting something on her. It's a smoke screen. If we never look at what is wrong with ourselves, we will just stir up a whole lot of smoke and leave.

This is the way many marriages go year after year, accusing each other and throwing things at each other, but never saying, "You know, you are right." You'll have your chance to bring up the issue that you want to confront your spouse about, but when you are being confronted is not the time to do it. It's a time to be quiet and say, "You're right. You nailed me. That's why I married you."

3. **Don't react to your spouse's hurt feelings with your own hurt feelings.**

Proverbs, chapter 15, verse 1 says, **A soft answer turns away wrath, but a harsh word stirs up anger.** When you react, you start throwing sarcastic barbs and comments to each other, which stir up anger. But if you will respond rather than react, you will turn away wrath and bring harmony and unity into your home.

Sometimes I ask myself before I respond or react to Wendy, "Do I want to stir up anger, or do I want to turn away wrath?" A soft answer turns away wrath, but harsh words stir it up.

**A soft answer turns away wrath,
but harsh words stir it up.**

135

One of the most famous stories in our first couple of years together, was a few days before we got married. I was in Bible school and we were finishing up the quarter. I was taking tests, involved in ministry with several Bible studies going on, and I was preaching every night.

Back then I had the attitude, "I never have a problem or a bad thought. I've got everything under control. I'm superman. I can do everything." I was feeling a lot of tension and stress. One of my friends asked me if I was uptight, and I said, "Uptight about what?" He started laughing. He said, "You're so out of control, man, you don't even know it."

As we were driving to the apartment we were getting ready to move into, I said to Wendy, "Man, I'm just frustrated." We got to squabbling about something and she got mad at me. She started reacting to my stress, anger, and frustration. We got out of the car. I had a bag of groceries, and I dropped a big bag of Cheetos on the sidewalk. I can't remember what she said to me, but I lost it. I said, "Fine," and kicked the Cheetos. Both ends exploded. We had cheese puffs all over the street.

We got married and about a month later I was out getting something from my car. My neighbor came by and asked, "How's everything?" "Fine." "Have a great wedding?" "It was great." He asked, "You been in athletics?" I said, "In high school I played a little bit of sports." He said, "Football, huh? You were a kicker?" I said, "No, I never was a kicker." He said, "Well, your dropkick sure is good." He started laughing and related how he had seen me kick the bag of Cheetos that exploded!

We have to be careful not to react. When your husband is stressed out at work, don't make the house more stressful. Don't add to the problem. Stay out of the hole so you can help him get out. When your wife is frustrated over the kids, it is not the time to counsel her on how she can be a better parent.

Most men are glad to be going to work where they deal with a few employees. They can fire them if they want to, but a mother can't fire her kids.

4. Talk to bring restoration rather than to prolong the disagreement.

Before you speak, ask yourself, "Will this bring restoration, or will it simply prolong the disagreement?" Some of us purposefully stir things up and keep them going day after day. It's a habit, a part of our flesh. We're so involved with competition, being right, and selfishness that we prolong the disagreement by the things we say.

5. Talk until you understand what your spouse is thinking.

To really understand why another person is thinking or feeling a certain way is very difficult. Wars are fought because people refuse to understand each other. We have cultural wars and racial hatred because we don't want to understand what someone else is going through. We hate people instead of really wanting to understand what is going on in their lives.

In some of our homes we get so frustrated with each other that we don't want to be around each other. And the Church world is no different than the natural world. God holds a different standard of accountability for those in a marriage covenant when you've got His Word and His Spirit. Don't throw in the towel. Hang in there until you understand.

In the Church world, many people are giving up on their marriage. God never throws in the towel on us. And we don't have that option. We are to talk and hang in there until we understand, and that may take a long time.

God never throws in the towel on us.

Wendy and I were twenty-two and twenty-four when we went into full-time ministry. We became senior pastors of a multi-million dollar ministry before we were thirty, with thousands of people looking to us for leadership. We had to improve our communication skills.

After many years of marriage, I'm starting to understand how Wendy thinks and feels. I consider our relationship to be above average in terms of communication, agreement, and the things we've been able to accomplish. And we are still working on our communication skills!

Application of Family Covenant Truths

Please answer each of these statements/questions using Chapter 12 as your source of information:

1. "Corrupt communication" is: _____
   _____
   _____
   _____

2. I will minister "grace" with my words, which means:
   _____
   _____
   _____

3. The Holy Spirit can be grieved by: _____
   _____
   _____
   _____

4. I will "put away" the five negative qualities listed in Ephesians 4:31 in *all* of my relationships, which are:

   a. _____
   b. _____
   c. _____
   d. _____
   e. _____

5. I will follow the three directives in Ephesians 4:32 with my mate, which are:

   a. _____

   b. _____

   c. _____

6. The five keys to more effective communication listed by the author are:

   a. _____
   _____

   b. _____
   _____

   c. _____
   _____

   d. _____
   _____

   e. _____
   _____

Living Purposefully and Accurately

Relationships are a major key in your life. In fact, how you relate to people will decide much about your destiny. Some people have said that in any job, regardless of what the responsibilities are, that job is 90 percent people skills and 10 percent technical things. Your ability to relate is a controlling factor in your life and in your destiny.

The key relationships in your life are the ones with your spouse and with your children. If you're divorced, you are dealing with extended family relationships. If you're preparing to be married, you are in the process of learning and developing new relationships. The relationship with your spouse and children is a key to all of your relationships and to your destiny. That is why it is so important that we get God's perspective on family life.

The relationship with your spouse and children is a key to all of your relationships and to your destiny.

One of the things that I have been working on through our media ministry is seminars where we can teach about building better relationships. We'll deal with family, but we will also deal with the relationships that we have on the job, at church, and in every part of life, because if people don't know how to have right relationships, they're going to suffer, they're going to struggle, and they're going to be miserable. The world can't teach you how to build right relationships.

The challenge that many of us face is that we have been trained to believe what a wife or a husband is to be from a worldly perspective. We've been trained what a mother or father should be from a worldly perspective. Now we're reading biblical truths, and to make a change to line up with a biblical perspective is called "renewing the mind." We're trying to renew our minds so that we get rid of the worldly perspective of marriage and family and take on a biblical perspective.

Romans 12:2 says:

> And do not be conformed to this world, but be transformed by the renewing of your mind, that you may prove what is that good and acceptable and perfect will of God.

If you don't change your way of thinking and you hang on to old paradigms, attitudes, thoughts, and beliefs that you didn't get from the Bible, you won't have God's will in that part of your life. It's only as you are transformed by the renewing of your mind that you can prove the perfect will of God. This is why we have people who truly love the Lord, but their marriage is failing and their kids are going off in the world. They haven't renewed their mind to the biblical perspective of family relationships.

Remember, the goal in parenting is to raise godly men and women who will go out and begin a new family that will affect our world for Christ. The goal is not to have enough kids so they can take care of you when you get old. If you follow biblical perspectives, you will have more than enough to take care of yourself and give to your kids and your grandkids when you get old.

If you are counting on your kids taking care of you when you are old, you are not a Bible person. You are a "leach" or a "moocher" and that's not Bible! The Bible way is to be able to bless everybody in your latter years because you have followed the biblical perspective.

You are not raising your kids to visit you every Thanksgiving and Christmas, or so they will make you feel good by bringing the grandkids over and telling them how great a parent you were. You're not raising them to get something. Instead, *you are raising them to invest something into the world for God's Kingdom.*

As parents, we get our satisfaction from seeing our kids impact the world for Christ. We are blessed and fulfilled by seeing them be a light in the darkness and salt in the earth, making a difference.

If we've done our job as parents, we aren't manipulating them to come and visit us or griping at them because they haven't called for six years. We are not controlling them with emotions, guilt, promises of inheritance, and all that junk. If you have been a part of that, *repent*, get saved, and act like a

Christian! Stop manipulating and controlling your adult kids. Stop expecting things from them and stop putting guilt and condemnation on them. Let them leave so they can cleave. And if you allow that, they'll probably call you more often, and they might even want to come and see you!

The reason I emphasize this point so hard is because most people do not have pure motives when raising their kids. They do not have biblical motives. They have worldly attitudes, which cause all kinds of confusion when they try to start a new family. It brings problems that I am dealing with in the counseling office with parents who won't let their adult kids go.

The cycle of manipulating and controlling parents must be broken. It starts with a proper perspective of family, which we talked about in Chapter 1.

I started my family the day I said "I do" to Wendy and she said "I do" to me. We are to leave father and mother and cleave to each other. Later, we added to our family — not a permanent addition, but a leased arrangement! At eighteen, nineteen, or twenty years of age, the lease is up. God says, "Cut them loose. Let them leave so they can cleave and start their own family."

As parents, our focus with our children from birth to age five is on *love and discipline and control*. From six to ten, it's on *giving them biblical perspectives*. We teach them to pray, to worship God, and to honor their elders. We teach them to do their homework and to be obedient and diligent.

Any person who says about their ten-year-old, "I want to let them make their own choice about religion," is literally turning them over to the devil. That thinking comes from secular humanism. God holds us as parents accountable for how we affect our young children. He says it would be better if a millstone were tied around our neck than to turn our children over to wickedness or lead them astray.

From ages eleven to fifteen, we *encourage and motivate* our youngsters to use what they have learned, and help them develop a sense of destiny, realizing that God has a plan for their life. From sixteen to twenty years of age, we *make sure they have internalized the godly things we have taught them*, and then we become their friend, by doing a lot more listening than talking.

It's not easy to go from being a teacher/trainer when they are six years old to a listener when they are sixteen, still trying to teach and train them like they are six. If we do that, we frustrate them and turn them off, and they think we are fuddy duddies! To continue to teach and train our kids when they are sixteen as if they are six is to provoke them to wrath (Ephesians 6:4).

How Do You Spend Your Time?

Ephesians 5:15 AMP says:

> Look carefully then how you walk! Live purpose-fully *and* worthily *and* accurately, not as the unwise *and* witless, but as wise (sensible, intelligent people).

For every meeting, every appointment, every relationship, everything you are involved in, ask yourself, "Is this purposeful? Is this worthy of my time, energy, and commitment? Is it accurate and in agreement with God's will for my life? Is it a part of God's plans and purposes for my life?

Most people function on what is urgent and what other people expect them to do. "Why did you go to that meeting?" "Well, so-and-so wanted me to go." "Did you want to go?" "No." "Why did you go?" "Well, you know, they really wanted me to." So you live by what others expect rather than by what you believe is God's will.

Wendy and I went to a conference where several work-shops were being held. I looked at the list of workshops

145

and said to Wendy, "I'm not going to any of those." She said, "We've got to go to some, because they are expecting us to go. And if we're not there, they will be mad and might say something to us." I said, "Wendy, do you want to go to any of those workshops?" She said, "No, I don't really want to go." I said, "Good, we are not going."

What we really wanted to do was just to be together as a couple and hang around the pool and talk, but we've got these expectations of us as the preacher and the pastor, and we're supposed to do what preachers and pastors do. Usually that means you don't have time for your wife or for yourself.

We were in this dilemma, and finally I said, "Look, if it's God's will that we be there, then we should go. But if it's not God's will, then we have no reason to go. Who cares what anybody thinks?"

> Making the very most of the time [buying up each opportunity], because the days are evil. Therefore do not be vague *and* thoughtless *and* foolish, but understanding *and* firmly grasping what the will of the Lord is.
>
> **Ephesians 5:16,17 AMP**

The fact that God tells you to understand His will for your life means you can. He wouldn't tell you to do something that's impossible. So it's possible to understand and firmly grasp what the will of the Lord is for your life and for your family. That's where you should focus and stay plugged in, keep your priorities right, your scheduling right, and your lifestyles right.

I break "living accurately and purposefully" into six categories: faith, fitness, family, fellowship, finances, and fun. Let's look briefly at each of these areas:

1. Faith

The focus here is our relationship with God. Anytime we say, "I don't have time for God, I don't have time for prayer or Bible study or meditation," we've got problems. Your family won't get what they need, your job won't get what it needs, and your life is not going to be what God wants it to be. For it to be all God wants it to be requires a good relationship with heaven. Your kids aren't getting what they need either if you don't have time for the Lord.

2. Fitness

If you aren't mentally and physically fit, your family won't get what it needs and your job won't get what it needs. To live accurately and purposefully, there must be time for exercise.

3. Family

To live accurately and purposefully, you must have time with your spouse. There will be seasons when you are ripping and running, very busy with the job, career, ministry, kids, whatever. Balance all this with time alone with your spouse.

When you don't let your kids interrupt your private time together as husband and wife and they see Mom and Dad as a strong, unified front, and they see themselves as second to Mom and Dad, they will feel secure. Something inside of them says, "We're healthy." But when they get in between Mom and Dad, they are insecure.

You also need family time with your children, both individually and as a group.

4. Fellowship

Fellowship for accurate and purposeful living refers to your church life — being a part of the family of God.

Psalm 92:13,14 says:

> Those who are planted in the house of the Lord shall flourish in the courts of our God. They shall still bear fruit in old age; they shall be fresh and flourishing.

5. Finances

Finances for accurate and purposeful living have to do with your job and your career. You spend more hours in this area than in any of the other five areas.

If my job ever becomes an issue between me and God, the job goes. If my job starts taking my mental and physical health, it goes. It's way behind family. If it starts destroying my family, the job goes. When your job starts taking the family time, *your priorities are out of whack,* and you are in trouble.

Anything on my job that would distract from my relationship with the house of God and my worship also has to go.

6. Fun

Work your fun times to include your wife and children.

Lord, from this day forth, help me to live with divine purpose and accuracy, with purity of heart, in pursuit of the destiny You have set before me. Help me to be a blessing to all the relationships that You intend to be a part of my life, in Jesus' name.

Application of Family Covenant Truths

Please answer each of these statements/questions using Chapter 13 as your source of information:

1. To "renew my mind" to a biblical perspective of marriage and family relationships, I will: _____

   _____

   _____

   _____

   _____

   _____

2. My primary goal in parenting is: _____

   _____

   _____

   _____

3. I am living purposefully and accurately by: _____

   _____

   _____

   _____

4. To be "planted" in the house of the Lord means:

   _____

   _____

   _____

   _____

Returning to Your First Love

R evelation, chapter 2, verse 2 says, "I know your works, your labor, your patience, and that you cannot bear those who are evil." Verses 4 and 5 continue, "Nevertheless I have *this* against you, that you have left your first love. Remember therefore from where you have fallen; repent and do the first works"....

In application to the church as a whole, many people get excited about the Lord, then church becomes a routine, and then people become religious rather than spiritual. They may be doing good things, but they aren't loving Jesus. They may be going through church routines, but it's a real drag to them.

Now, let's apply this principle to family life. Before the marriage, there is a short time of good communication, communion, and excitement about the relationship. After the marriage, you lose your first love and begin to function through the marriage routine, not really enjoying the marriage relationship.

When we were dating, I opened the door for Wendy. I took her out to dinner, and we went for walks. We talked and did many things to show our affection and love to each other.

Speaking for men as a whole, we did whatever we had to do, but then, after years of marriage, we left our first love and fell in love with our jobs, the yard, the boat, our fishing poles, our baseball games, and all of our activities.

Now we say to our wife, "I don't have time to go out on a date." Or, "We can't afford to go out to dinner." You could afford it when you didn't have anything. You have left your first love and now you're in love with all this other stuff. So the Lord says to you, "Remember, therefore, from where you have fallen. Remember what brought you together. Remember what attracted you to that person. Remember what caused you to want to be married. Remember where you started in your relationship. Remember those good things."

It's easy to get so focused on everything that's wrong in your marriage that you completely forget the things that are right. Remember therefore from where you have fallen and repent. That means to admit that you are wrong, that you've missed it: "Honey, my priorities are wrong. I have been selfish. I confess my sin." Now, Jesus didn't say that's all there is to it, because to *remember* and to *repent* doesn't change anything.

It's easy to get so focused on everything that's wrong in your marriage that you completely forget the things that are right.

As men, we are good at saying what we have to say to get through a discussion. We are sincere, but some of us don't follow up after that. The Lord said, after you remember and repent, **Do the first works** (Revelation 2:5).

What are the first works? Romance, sweet talk, calling, buying things, taking her places. Do the first works. Continue to do what brought you together so that you can continue to stay together. Continue to do what made you fall in love so you can continue to fall in love. Do the first works again.

One of the most common concepts in the world is that you can "fall out of love." They say, "I lost that love feeling." In the church, we fall into that same mentality or trap, believing that the love is gone. Somehow we think love is like a cloud. It drifts in and it drifts out. It's like the sun. It comes and it goes. That's a worldly, unscriptural concept. You don't lose love. *You choose to stop loving.* You leave your first love, but you can get it back by doing the first works over.

Here's how to get the love back: **Nevertheless I have** *this* **against you, that you have left your first love** (Revelation 2:4). See, the love didn't leave. You left it! You can get it back if you **repent and do the first works** (v. 5).

I can't tell you how many times I've had a spouse tell me, "The love is gone, but it's not my fault. I don't know how it happened. What do you expect me to do?"

When people say, "I'm questioning whether it was God's will that we got married in the first place," what they're saying is, "I choose *not* to love." Part of love says, "I believe God wants us to be together. I choose to love you as if God brought us together." That's a choice, a decision. As long as we choose to love, we will love in our relationships. But as soon as we back away and leave our first love, then it's gone.

We can repent and do the first works and get right back to the first love.

We leave our first love on the inside long before it is evident on the outside. Lack of communication, anger, bitterness, and unforgiveness are going on internally, which cause us to leave our first love inside. Then it is manifested outwardly. We must regularly examine and, when necessary, repent and change and do those first works to keep our first love alive.

What are some of the first works that you did to create and enter into that first love? You probably asked your spouse out for a date. You went to lunch or to dinner. (Wendy and I had a chauffeur on our first date — we took the Metro bus!) You probably talked about everything. You looked deep into each other's eyes. You were not reading the newspaper or a magazine when you talked. You were involved and you talked and talked. You wrote love letters and notes to each other. You sent flowers. When one of you went away on a business trip, the one remaining at home didn't think of all their faults and weaknesses. Instead, they thought only about the positive, warm, good things they brought into your life and the things you appreciated about them.

Then, of course, you were nice to her mom, selling yourself to her. You dressed up, at least to some degree. You used deodorant, cologne, etc. You thought about them first.

What happens when we lose the love feeling? We smell like last week's garbage can. We forget to open her car door when we go to the restaurant. Rather than open the door, we yell, "Hurry up!" Then, when we look at the other people sitting in the restaurant, we can tell the ones who are dating. They are just looking at each other and talking in between bites. We can tell the ones who are married, because they don't even look at each other and they're spaced out.

The good news is, we can change all that and regain our first love. *Repent* means to change. Do the first works and you will regenerate that first love. We need to be honest with ourselves. If we have stopped doing first works — thinking about the other person, planning good things, talking with them, being interested, looking for ways to bless them, and doing little things they like — we are losing our first love.

Four Ways To Keep Your Love Alive

Let's look at some of the ways to keep the marriage relationship lasting, fun, and fulfilling. Many people stay married after they've lost their first love. They don't get a divorce, but they're like two strangers living in the same house. Your goal should not be just to stay married. It should be to have some fun and to be fulfilled. Why have a miserable existence? Here are four ideas to keep your first love alive for all of your married life.

1. **Plan time to talk.** You have to plan for a time to talk just like you plan for an appointment at your office, to wash the car, or to mow the grass. Make a schedule and figure out ways that you can talk. Set up a date, go for a drive, go for a walk, plug in and pay attention and talk.

"Well, I don't feel like it." I really don't give two hoots about your feelings! What I mean is, when feelings run your life, you will generally feel bad. But when you do what is right, regardless of how you feel, you will generally feel good. How many times have you not felt like praying? You prayed anyway and when you were done, you really felt good about praying. How many times have you not felt like exercising, but you did it anyway? When you were done, you really felt good about it. *Don't let your feelings run your marriage.* Do what is right for your marriage, then feelings will follow.

2. **Keep prayer and the Word alive in your marriage.**

Now, I didn't say to have a prayer program or a Bible reading plan, a prayer time or a time to share the Word, but have a prayer life and a Word life. The issue is to keep prayer and the Word of God alive in your marriage.

You need to be praying for your children, your career, your ministry, your life, your friends, for every part of your being. Pray for healing if someone in your family is sick. Pray for finances and the challenges you are facing. Share the Word, talk about it, read it, and discuss it. If prayer and the Word are not alive in your marriage, then you are living a carnal life, and God can't do much in a carnal marriage.

You may say, "My husband doesn't want to talk about the Bible." Then share with him the exciting things you heard today in the Word. For example, "I was reading the Word today and God was talking about how Jesus took our sickness. I just realized I don't have to try to get healed. Isn't that great?"

Don't call your prayer life and your Bible life "a quiet time." Man, if you are in touch with God, you should have a shouting time! You should be running around your house sometimes. You should be speaking the Word. Quiet time creates an attitude that when you are spiritual, you are dead. It's just a term, but I don't use it. Quiet time to me is taking a nap. We need the Word and we need prayer to be <u>alive</u> in our homes. It doesn't have to be formal, although it can be. It doesn't have to be a program, although it can be. As a spouse, you are responsible to keep prayer and the Word alive in your marriage.

We need the Word and we need prayer to be *alive* in our homes.

---

3. Have goals, dreams, and visions that you are working toward together for your marriage, your ministry, your home, and your children.

The battles you are fighting, fight them together. The mountains you are climbing, climb them together. And the challenges you are going after, go after them together. If you're fighting *with* each other, you won't have time to fight *against* each other. If you're working together to reach goals, dreams, and visions, you won't have time to worry about all the little nit-picky things that so often destroy marriages.

4. Remember, your body, as much as your soul and spirit, is a part of your relationship.

Your body is a part of the marriage relationship, but not just in a sexual way. There are three ways your body is a part of this relationship:

First, your body is a part of this relationship when it comes to your health. If you're not healthy, it affects your marriage. If you're sick, weak, down, or struggling with your health, that affects your marriage. It takes life out of your marriage. So keep yourself healthy, which has to do with eating and exercise.

Second, your appearance affects your marriage. It affects your self-esteem, so keep yourself sharp, dress well, and look good. Guys, get rid of your 1967 tie! Your wife has learned to accept your ugly self, but she sure would feel better if you looked sharp! If it wasn't important, why didn't God just make everything gray?

Third, your sex life is an area of your body that is involved in the marriage relationship. Keep it fun and fulfilling.

Four Things for Your "Never Do" List

1. **Never walk away from a conversation.**

In other words, a fight, a discussion, a disagreement, whatever you call it — don't walk away from it. Exceptions would be if you have to put the kids to bed, go to work, or do some other activity that you have scheduled. Agree to talk more later, but never just walk away from a conversation.

Sometimes we don't walk away, but we just sit there. "Are you going to say anything else?" "No, I've got nothing else to say. What good would it do? I'm talking to the walls." There is more than one way to leave a conversation.

Always remember, when you leave a conversation, you have sown the seed for division. Every time you leave, slam the door, won't talk anymore, you sow another seed for division. It's practice for leaving for good.

2. **Never talk about, joke about, or focus on your spouse's weaknesses.**

Never talk to a friend about what you don't like about your spouse. Every sitcom lauds that, but we are never to participate in it. If your friend at the office jokes about something with his wife that he doesn't like, you need to say, "Brother, you should thank God for a woman who would marry a chump like you!"

When the guys are joking about women or making jokes about their wives, you need to be one who does not participate, but instead say, "Man, you'd better get home to that woman, because if you keep this up, one day she won't be there. Only then will you realize what you've lost."

3. **Never allow other relationships to come ahead of your marriage relationship.**

Don't allow another relationship to become your emotional crutch — where you get your attention, your love, and you share your feelings. I don't care if it's your mother, your father, your sister, your brother, your next door neighbor, the milkman, or your own kids. *Never allow another relationship to take first place.*

Many lesbian relationships started with a woman saying, "I could share so much more with this woman than I could with my husband." Many homosexual relationships started out where the guy said, "We talked at the golf course and we had such a camaraderie." He loved his golfing buddy, because he let that relationship become more important — it took first place over his marriage.

Sometimes moms and dads talk more to their kids than they do to each other. Never, never, never let another relationship take first place ahead of the marriage relationship.

4. **Never make your spouse the enemy.**

Have you ever heard any of these comments? "If only they'd change, everything would be okay." "If they would just do this." "They are making things hard." "He's the problem." "She's the problem." Don't make your spouse the enemy, because he or she is *not* the problem. The enemy may be using them, demonic spirits may be controlling them, it may seem like hell in the house, but that spouse is not your enemy.

In the final three chapters, we'll go into more depth about the biblical way to raise champion children.

Application of Family Covenant Truths

Please answer each of these statements/questions using Chapter 14 as your source of information:

1. Some of the things that are "right" about my mate are:

   _____

   _____

   _____

   _____

   _____

2. One area in my marriage relationship that still needs improvement is: _____

   _____

   _____

   I am praying the following Scripture promises over this area: _____

   _____

   _____

   _____

3. Some of the first works I need to do in my marriage relationship are: _____

   _____

   _____

   _____

   _____

   _____

4. Some of the "causes" for leaving my first love are:

_____

_____

_____

_____

5. Four ways to keep love alive in my marriage relationship are:

a. _____

_____

b. _____

_____

c. _____

_____

d. _____

_____

6. Four things on my "never do" list for my marriage relationship are:

a. _____

_____

b. _____

_____

c. _____

_____

d. _____

_____

Raising Champion Children

You shall teach them [God's Word] diligently to your children, and shall talk of them when you sit in your house, when you walk by the way, when you lie down, and when you rise up.

Deuteronomy 6:7

N otice, teaching our children isn't something that just happens in Sunday school or in their school classrooms. It's something that happens every day on a continual basis — when we get up in the morning, go to bed at night, talk and sit in our home, or when we walk or travel.

We are teaching our children the Word of God, the ways of God, and the principles of God continually. Teaching and training our children must be a *lifestyle*.

If your prayer is a prayer time and not a prayer life, then you won't be able to teach your children how to pray. If your Christianity is a quiet time and not a life in the Spirit, you won't teach your children how to walk with God.

If church is Sundays and Wednesdays, and not daily, then you'll never teach your children to know the Lord.

When Christianity isn't daily, it isn't real. When it is occasional, most of it is hypocritical and phony. The world in general rejects Christianity that is not incorporated into everyday life.

When you get up in the morning, talk with your kids about how the Lord will lead them that day, the good things they will be doing, the relationships they will be building, and how to treat their friends using godly principles. After going for a walk, talk to them about the neighbors and about how to pray for them to be saved. Talk about God's protection, how the Lord leads, and how His angels are encamped around about us, as described in Psalm 91.

There is a constant opportunity to teach and train our children if we, as parents, have the discipline to plug into it. Christianity has to be a "lifestyle."

Deuteronomy, chapter 6, verse 8, goes on to say:

> **"You shall bind them** [God's Word] **as a sign on your hand, and they shall be as frontlets between your eyes."**

In other words, "Whatever you look at, make sure that it is biblical and that you have a holy, spiritual, godly perspective."

The Word is to influence every part of our lives. **"You shall write them on the doorposts of your house and on your gates"** (Deuteronomy 6:9). You can put Scriptures on the walls of your home. Wendy and I have Scriptures and plaques on the walls of our home, but that's not the real meaning of this verse. It means everything that happens in the home needs to be ordered by the Lord and be in line with the Word.

Everything that happens in the
home needs to be ordered by the
Lord and be in line with the Word.

> "So it shall be, when the Lord your God brings
> you into the land of which He swore to your fathers, to
> Abraham, Isaac, and Jacob, to give you large and beau-
> tiful cities which you did not build, houses full of all
> good things, which you did not fill, hewn-out wells
> which you did not dig, vineyards and olive trees which
> you did not plant — when you have eaten and are full."
> Deuteronomy 6:10,11

Moses is speaking specifically to Israel as they take over the promised land, but it's also part of the promise of God to all of His children. He wants us to prosper, and He takes pleasure in our prosperity (Psalm 35:27).

Verse 12 says, "*Then* **beware, lest you forget the Lord who brought you out of the land of Egypt, from the house of bondage.**" Beware! Do you know people who have been blessed, then they bought a big boat and no longer had time for church? They got so blessed they got a Winnebago and now they don't come to church during the summer months anymore. They got so blessed they don't have to work hard, so they are running around the world and don't have time to be a part of the work of the Lord anymore. You see, they have forgotten their love for God and where their abundance came from.

We teach our children by the Word, which affects everything we are and everything we do. Discipline is a part of this balanced life we are teaching our children. In our generation there has been an emphasis on love, allowing a child to express himself. We have emphasized mercy and grace to the point where parents have the concept that raising children means just understanding them, loving them, allowing them to express themselves, giving them the room to grow up and find out who they are, and accepting them the way they are. We need to understand that love, mercy, and grace have no meaning to a child without discipline, judgment, and righteousness.

Let me say it like this: Forgiveness, mercy, and grace have no meaning to the person who feels he has done nothing wrong. If you say to a homosexual who was raised as a heathen, "I want you to know I love you and accept you," he's going to say, "What? Where are you coming from?" He has no understanding of what you are saying. In fact, he is offended by what you said because he doesn't think he is doing anything wrong.

If you say to a drunkard, "God loves you and He forgives you," he will say, "For what?" He has no concept of righteousness, because he has no concept of judgment and justice. He can't understand forgiveness and mercy, so he looks at you as if you're some kind of nut.

When we say to someone in the world, "You need to get saved," they say, "Saved from what?" If there is no concept of sin, there can be no understanding of salvation.

If you don't teach your children righteousness, justice, and judgment, what is good and what is bad, what is right and what is wrong, and discipline them to live by the rules of God's Word, they will never understand love, mercy, and forgiveness. They are being raised up with anger and hostility because they have no concept to understand these qualities of life.

Parents who think they are being so kind and good to their children by not spanking or disciplining them, giving them whatever they want, and allowing them to say whatever they want, are hurting them tragically. They will run into somebody about the time they are six years old who won't let them express what they feel and who will deal with them harshly. The child won't know how to respond, because you, the parent, haven't disciplined them.

Without an understanding of obedience and discipline, a child has no understanding of disobedience.

God's Thoughts About Disobedience

God has some strong things to say about disobedience. In I Samuel 15, the prophet Samuel spoke to Saul, Israel's first king:

> "When you *were* little in your own eyes, *were* you not head of the tribes of Israel? And did not the Lord anoint you king over Israel? Now the Lord sent you on a mission, and said, 'Go, and utterly destroy the sinners, the Amalekites, and fight against them until they are consumed.' Why then did you not obey the voice of the Lord? Why did you swoop down on the spoil, and do evil in the sight of the Lord?"
>
> And Saul said to Samuel, "But I have obeyed the voice of the Lord, and gone on the mission on which the Lord sent me, and brought back Agag king of Amalek; I have utterly destroyed the Amalekites. But the people took of the plunder, sheep and oxen, the best of the things which have been utterly destroyed, to sacrifice to the Lord your God in Gilgal."
>
> I Samuel 15:17-21

People are still trying to negotiate and make deals with God rather than obey. Here's an example: "I'm going to use the tithe for myself now, Lord, but I'll do something with it that will honor You and will show the world how good You are. When I get caught up on the bills, I'll give You double tithes."

> So Samuel said: "Has the Lord *as great* delight in burnt offerings and sacrifices, as in obeying the voice of the Lord? Behold, to obey is better than sacrifice, *and* to heed than the fat of rams. For rebellion *is as* the sin of witchcraft, and stubbornness *is as* iniquity and idolatry. Because you have rejected the word of the Lord, He also has rejected you from *being* king."
>
> I Samuel 15:22,23

For rebellion is as the sin of witchcraft, and stubbornness is as iniquity and idolatry (I Samuel 15:23).

As a result of King Saul's disobedience, the kingdom was ripped out of his hands.

If we don't raise our children to be submissive and obedient, to obey the Bible, to be disciplined and able to control their flesh, and do what God has commanded them to do, we are turning them over to witchcraft, idolatry, and all kinds of sin.

The more rebellion that we allow in our society, the more satanic things become popular. Today we've got entire television stations committed to wicked spirits, new age spirits, and psychics. People are being caught up in these spirits. The root of these activities is *rebellion against God.*

As parents we are responsible to raise our kids with a submissive, obedient spirit. The Holy Spirit through Samuel said that rebellion is as the sin of witchcraft. We open our children's lives up to wicked spirits when we don't raise them in the Word of God and in obedience, submission, and discipline.

If you, as a parent, took part in wicked rock concerts and passed it off as a light thing, I would ask you, where are you today versus where you could be in the Lord, in your family, in your business? How much did it cost you to open your life to that kind of evil influence?

We've got to raise our children up with a different spirit — the Spirit of the Lord, the Spirit of the Champion of all champions — and live a disciplined life ourselves, then pass it on to our children. When we live a life of discipline, righteousness, judgment, and justice, then there is a context for love, acceptance, mercy, and grace. Everything makes sense to our children when they have that right context.

When we live a life of discipline, righteousness, judgment, and justice, then there is a context for love, acceptance, mercy, and grace.

A disciplined life can be built on a foundation of moral character. God judges us based on character, and character has nothing to do with personality. I know some guys who have the personality of a dial tone, but they have great character. Charisma won't get you to God's blessing, but character will. Real success comes from moral character — the beliefs and the attitudes that cause you to be an honest person when no one is looking. It causes you to be a person of integrity when you don't have to be. It causes you to be biblically right, whether anyone knows or not.

Moral character must be in our lives before we can build discipline. Character is seen in how you respect and honor authority and in your honesty with authority figures.

Our children, no matter what kind of personality they have, can be blessed by God if they have moral character. Sometimes we think, "My child is not going to do very good, because he's so quiet." That has nothing to do with whether he succeeds or not. The controlling factor is *character*.

Let's briefly look at five levels of authority in relationship to building moral character in a child:

1. Governmental or Civic Authority

Romans 13:1 says, **Let every soul be subject to the governing authorities. For there is no authority except from God, and the authorities that exist are appointed by God.**

Let's say you are driving down the road and the sign says 60 miles an hour. You are going 70 and your children say, "Dad, how come you're speeding?" You get stopped by a policeman and your response to your children is, "Well, you know, the cops have to make a buck. They just give people a hard time."

You wonder why the next day when you say to your son, "I want your room picked up," he says, "No, I don't have time, Dad." You're thinking, "What's wrong with this kid? Doesn't he respect authority?" No, he doesn't, because you taught him not to.

You are driving down the road at 75 miles an hour, and all of a sudden you see a policeman. As you hit the brakes to slow down, you say, "I hope he didn't see me."

The next day at home, you walk into your child's bedroom, and he stuffs something under the bed. You ask, "What's under there?" "Nothing," he responds. "What do you mean, nothing?" He says, "Nothing." You find out he has taken something you told him not to take. You ask, "How could you do that? Didn't I tell you not to get into my things?"

By your behavior, you are training them that you do what you're not supposed to do as long as you don't get caught. Too many of us live by not getting caught. But when you really respect authority, you'll respect authority whether they are watching or not. As parents, when we break a rule, we need to admit that we are wrong.

If fifteen cars are all going the same speed and you get pulled over by a policeman (with the kids in the car), the test is on. If that were me, how would I respond? I would say, "Yes, sir. Thank you. You're right, I was speeding. I deserve a ticket. Thank you." It happened to me and that's what I said.

Inside of me, I thought mercy and grace could have gone a long way, but what I'm thinking and feeling has to submit to what is right. As a parent, I must respect authority if I want my children to respect authority. If I gripe and complain, what are they going to do?

As a parent, I must respect authority if I want my children to respect authority.

When the policeman pulled away and I got my ticket, the kids said, "Man, Dad, how come he gave you a ticket?" "Because he's a policeman, and he did the right thing." "Yeah, but he didn't have to." "Well, I was hoping he wouldn't, but he did and that's okay. He's doing his job and I'll drive better because of it."

See, we have to live what we are trying to teach our children. We can't speed or disrespect authority and talk bad and then wonder why our kids mess up.

2. Parental Authority

Moral character is built into a child who is taught to honor and respect parental authority.

Ephesians 6:1-3 says:

> **Children, obey your parents in the Lord, for this is right.** *"Honor your father and mother,"* **which is the first commandment with promise:** *"That it may be well with you and you may live long on the earth."*

As parents, our relationship with our children will grow in phases. From approximately age twenty on, we can be friends and buddies. Obviously, a parent is always a friend to his children, there is a closeness and an intimacy and they have fun together, but when we're trying to teach and train them, if we allow our friendship to compromise our position as a parent, we will hurt the children. Too many parents are more concerned about their child liking them than they are about training them properly.

I've been in the spot where my children needed discipline and I'm wondering how they are going to feel about it. As a parent, it's not my job to worry about how they're going to feel about it. But it is my job to make sure they are trained properly. If I'm more concerned with them liking me, I will start compromising and allowing them to slide and in the end they will hate me because I didn't prepare them to be successful in life.

Proverbs 30:17 speaks of disrespect for parents: **The eye** *that* **mocks** *his* **father, and scorns obedience to** *his* mother, the ravens of the valley will pick it out, and the young eagles will eat it.

In Romans, chapter 1, one of the descriptions of those who are in rebellion to godliness and righteousness is "disobedience to parents" (Romans 1:30). Other Scriptures say that those who hate their parents or who shame them will be cursed.

3. Respect for the Elderly

I used to have the attitude that if you called an adult by their first name and let the kids do that, it helped them feel closer to you. All of a sudden I realized it wasn't working.

We are building moral character into our children as we teach them to use "Yes, ma'am," "Yes, sir," "Pastor so-and-so," and titles for those in authority and who are older, rather than using first names.

A Jewish proverb says that caring for the aged is akin to caring for God Himself. Some of the ways to teach our children to show respect to the elderly are allowing the elderly to go through the door first and to give an older person our seat on the bus if it is full. As a man, give the lady a seat. The key is, our heart attitude should be to honor the aged.

I want my children to respect other people. If they need to talk to me when I am talking or praying with someone, we have developed what I call "the interrupt rule." They can put a hand on my side or grab my hand. This means, "Dad, I'm touching you because I want to talk to you as soon as you get a breath, an opportunity, a place in the conversation. I need to ask you something."

The person with whom I am talking can finish their sentence, and then I'll say, "Just a moment. Let me get a message from my son, then you and I will continue our conversation." My child is not only respecting me, he is respecting the other person.

A child who yells, "Dad...Dad" and interrupts, lacks parental respect as well as respect for others. He thinks everything should stop for him. Child-centered parenting produces "me-centered" lives.

Child-centered parenting produces "me-centered" lives.

Wendy and I have a rule in our home that if the bedroom door is closed, we are talking and you must knock. If we answer, that means we will chat with you right then. If we don't answer, that means we can't talk right then. Our kids have learned to respect this rule. Obviously, the rule does not apply if there is an emergency.

If we are in the living room and we are talking or we are at the kitchen table talking, the kids will come up and stand there for a minute. We do not allow them to barge in and announce that they are now in control of the house. Don't allow your kids to grow up with that spirit.

"The interrupt rule" may be one way that you can teach respect and honor and still be able to take care of business in a positive way.

Some parents have allowed the shyness of their child to be an excuse for disrespect. Even if they are shy, they can still say "thank you" and be courteous.

4. Respect for Siblings and Peers

We are to treat each person, including brothers and sisters, with dignity and respect. There are times when brothers and sisters are going to wrestle, pick on each other, and play. We're not talking about playing and having fun and being kids, but in their dealings with each other, they must love one another. If we raise them to love each other and treat each other with respect and dignity, that's the way they will live. That's moral character. That's the way my family is and there are no other options.

That doesn't mean they are going to do it automatically, but they will accept it as reality and will live that way. I've had parents come to me and say, "You know, I just don't know how I'm ever going to get my children to love each other. There is so much strife and anger in our home. I won't talk to my sister and my brother won't talk to me. I'm afraid my children are going to be the same way."

If that's the way you think, they probably will be like that, because in your mind strife and anger are optional. In your mind you are hoping they will love each other, but it's not a reality.

Your children will rise to your level of expectation. If you expect them to treat their siblings with respect and dignity, they will. If you just hope they do, they probably won't.

In that process of teaching our children to treat their peers and siblings with respect and dignity, we teach them that life is not fair. It's not fair that your sister goes on three special dates this week — the women's breakfast, the fashion show, and a special date with a girlfriend who has concert tickets.

However, it's also not fair that you have a mom and a dad, and there are a whole lot of kids in your school that don't have both parents. It's also not fair that you live in America and there are millions of kids who don't. It's also not fair that you get to go to school every day in a nice, warm car. There are literally millions of kids living on dirt floors, hoping and fighting for a meal each day.

5. Property of Others

Moral character is developed when we have respect for the property of others. One of the Ten Commandments is that we not steal (Exodus 20:15). This verse is also talking about how we treat the property of others. Not only should we not steal, we shouldn't break it, deface it, or misuse it. We are to treat the property of others with care and concern.

Why do we have a graffiti problem in public bathrooms in almost every city in America? Because of children raised without moral character.

You're wondering, "Is it a sin to paint on a wall?" The sin is in not having respect for other people's property. Painting on the wall is just a manifestation of the lack of moral character. God doesn't look at what you wrote on the bathroom wall. He looks at your heart to see what makes you think you can do that.

Let's get real nit-picky for a little test. You are in a phone booth and you are writing down a phone number. You don't have any paper, so you rip a page out of the phone book. After all, there are thousands of pages in it.

I come into the phone booth after you and I can't find a number in the book because that page is torn out. Someone with no moral character didn't care about the property that was for me as much as it was for them.

One of the Ten Commandments was just broken: "Thou shalt not steal." A page out of the phone book is no different than $1, $10, or $50. We are talking about moral character. When children see their parents compromise godly principles, it weakens and damages their moral character.

Another illustration of respecting or disrespecting the property of others is when you're in a parking lot and you open your door. Bang! You've got an old rattletrap and you just put a dent in the car next to yours. You say, "I can't tell my insurance company because my insurance premiums are already so high I can't hardly afford them. What am I going to do? God, forgive me."

The Lord forgives you for banging the guy's car, but He doesn't forgive you for having no character. If you've got to work overtime or sell your heap to pay for the dent, do it. It's better to keep your character than to be a fake, a phony, and a liar with no respect for other people's property.

Genesis 1:26 says, "Let **Us** make **man** in **Our image, according to Our likeness;** <u>let them have dominion</u>".... The first thing that happens when we become like God is we are to take dominion. So the first word out of our little God-like creatures is "mine." Right?

Until I renewed my mind in this area, I always thought children were saying "mine" out of selfishness, but that's not true. They are saying "mine" out of their God-like desire for dominion. Now, their desire for dominion will become selfish, greedy, and perverted if we don't teach them moral character. But if we teach them moral character, their desire for dominion will be godly.

As we teach our children to respect other people's property, we teach them the dominion principle. The city has dominion over certain parks and roads, but they allow us to enjoy them and use them. I don't have the right to put a piece of paper on the road or in the park because someone has dominion over that property and someone else is to enjoy it. I am violating their dominion and the other people's right to enjoy it by putting my piece of paper there.

So I teach my kids as they grow up, "We don't litter," not because someone is watching and you can get a ticket, but because it violates the principles of dominion and other people's rights. We have to raise our children to understand dominion. Children will have dominion over some things, and we can't expect them to share everything.

We put toys in a particular part of our house that are for everybody. If they get broken, we learn how to forgive. If they get lost, we learn how to forgive and forget. But there are those things over which we have taken dominion, whether it's a special toy, a collection, clothing, or a particular item that is valuable.

Don't require your children to share their special valuables. At the same time, don't leave the "valuable" items in the middle of the floor with twenty-three children running around it, with you saying, "You can't touch it." We must teach our children how to guard those items over which they have dominion.

It's just my opinion, but I believe when you drive down the road in your rattletrap jalopy that hasn't been washed for the last five years, it's got dents, the bumpers are falling off, and Jesus stickers are holding the doors shut, you are violating my rights! You're saying, "I don't care what anybody thinks. I'm a mess. What you think means nothing to me."

I understand that we're all at various places in our growth in the Lord, but my attitude is, even if you've got an old jalopy, you should keep it as clean and shiny and respectful as possible. Why? If you don't shine it, why should God give you anything better? If you're saying, "I need a Scripture on that," I can give you one. Luke, chapter 16, verse 10 says, **"He who *is* faithful in *what is* least is faithful also in much; and he who is unjust in *what is* least is unjust also in much."**

It used to be that when I drove a rental car, I wasn't as careful as when I drove my own car. When I began to understand that people with no moral character usually don't take proper care of rental items, I changed my attitude and my actions. Today I have respect and honor for other people's property, and I've made a decision to treat the rental car just as if it were my own car.

Why do children lose things and not care? Leave the car doors open? Won't bring their bicycles in out of the rain? Because they're not being raised with moral character to care about other people's property or even their own.

My dad raised us to take care of things, and we always kept things neat and clean. He was very disciplined in this area of his life. He was a carpenter so he had lots of tools. We could use the tools as long as we used them properly and put them away when we were done with them.

One day Dad's handsaw disappeared. I swore up and down I hadn't used it. Not me! About a week later he was out in the pasture doing something with the horses, and he looked around my fort that I had been building. There was his handsaw, only now it was covered with rust. He walked up the driveway with his rusty handsaw and said, "Guess where I found this?" Right then I remembered that I had been using it. I was disciplined severely.

Children who are not raised with a respect for the property of others are the ones who are throwing their garbage around the parks and banging and denting someone else's car in the parking lot. They're the ones who don't care about stealing pencils, paper, or whatever from the office. They have no moral character.

To raise champion children requires a decision and follow-through by the parents to build moral character into them by teaching, training, and discipline.

Application of Family Covenant Truths

Please answer each of these statements/questions using Chapter 15 as your source of information:

1. To make teaching and training children a "lifestyle" means: _____

   _____

   _____

   _____

   _____

   _____

2. The basis or source from which I teach my children is:

   _____

   _____

3. To raise my children with a submissive and obedient spirit, I will: _____

   _____

   _____

   _____

   _____

   _____

4. Moral character is: _____

   _____

   _____

   _____

   _____

5. The five levels of authority that must be dealt with in developing moral character in my child are:

a. _____

b. _____

c. _____

d. _____

e. _____

Children Will Rise to the Level of Parental Expectation

Children will always rise to the level of expectation and to the example of their parents. Negative parenting undermines the goal of raising godly, moral, champion children. I believe every parent wants their children to be filled with honesty and integrity. They have character values they want their children to live by.

Negative parenting includes threats, repetition, and inconsistencies. You say to the child, "Come over here and be still." He continues to run around, touch things, and do what he was doing, ignoring your directive. You repeat, "I said, come over here and be still. I'm not going to say it again. Come over here and be still. If you don't come over here and be still, you're in big trouble. All right, that's it. I told you for the last time, come over here and be still."

Now you are an example of everything you don't want your child to be — a liar. "I'm not going to say it again." But you did say it again and again, so you lied.

To threaten, repeat, and be inconsistent undermines what we are trying to accomplish with our children.

Negative parenting includes bribing or trading: "If you'll do this, I'll do that." "If you'll be good, I'll buy you some candy." "If you'll sit still in the grocery cart, I'll get you a prize."

An example of reversing this situation, turning it to a positive experience, would be, if the child sits still and obeys and you buy them a prize, when you leave the grocery store, you say, "You were so good. I am proud of the way you acted. Here is a special prize." Rewarding good behavior is very positive, but bribing to get the good behavior is very negative.

Rewarding good behavior is very positive, but bribing to get the good behavior is very negative.

Negative parenting would also be to raise your child to always think in terms of, "How can I get them to give me what I want before I do what they want?" When a little girl grows up who has been taught this way, she will become a manipulating wife. And a young boy taught this way will become a controlling husband.

Negative parenting involves "negotiating" with your child in the midst of conflict. When you are in a conflict with your child is not a time to negotiate. Let's say you want your child to sit still and they won't sit still, but they will stand still. You say, "Okay, close enough." No, that's negative parenting.

One hundred percent obedience is what you should expect. Anything less is a compromise.

One hundred percent obedience is what you should expect. Anything less is a compromise.

When you speak to your child in a way that requires an answer or an action, always expect complete and immediate obedience *the first time.* You say, "You've got to be kidding me." Remember, your child will rise to the level of expectation and example that you, as a parent, set for him or her. The child will figure out what you expect. If you expect them to obey the third time, they will wait until the third time to obey. If you expect them to obey the fifth time, they will wait until the fifth time to obey. If you expect them to obey when your face is red and there is a stick in your hand, they'll wait for the signal! Whatever you expect is what you'll get.

What is the difference between obedience the first time and obedience with a red face and a stick in hand? Nothing! It's just what you expect. You're not going to change what a child thinks you expect overnight. As you put new guidelines into practice, inform them, "Here is the way it's going to be," and then begin to enforce a new level of obedience.

The goal for positive parenting of champion children and for establishing moral character is that when you speak to your child in a way that requires an answer or an action, *expect complete and immediate obedience the first time.* You say, "Go clean your room." When you go upstairs, the room should be clean. You don't expect the child to throw everything in the closet, nor do you expect him or her to ignore your command. You don't expect the child to do half of it and hope it will be enough. *Expect complete and immediate obedience.* That means, never give a command unless you intend for it to be obeyed.

As parents, we have to take a look at ourselves and decide, "Am I going to say only what I really want the child to do?" Only then can we expect complete and first-time obedience.

As adults, God only says what He really wants us to do. If we don't obey it, then we are in disobedience. There is nothing in The Book that God commanded where He meant "if we feel like it." If you expect your children to obey you, then your example should be complete obedience to God. If you don't obey God, how can you expect your children to obey you?

Remember, children will only rise to the level of parental expectation and example. They know if Mom and Dad are obedient. The worst thing about being a parent is to see your child mirror everything you wish you weren't!

Never give a command unless you intend for it to be obeyed. You may provide warning and a time for preparation. For instance, if your kids are playing or are in the middle of a video, don't say, "All right, you're going to bed right now. Let's get going." The kids go, "What? Wait a minute. What time is it?" They don't function well when you walk in with surprises. Give them warnings. "In fifteen minutes we're going to bed. In ten minutes the television is going off."

Have you ever said "no" to your child, and then they ask again and you wonder, "Why did I say 'no' to that?" "Dad, can I go over to Bob's?" "No." "Why not?" "Because I said so." We give idiot commands and we also give idiot "no's." By that I mean, we give it no thought.

If you're not sure how to answer, don't answer. Instead, you can just say, "Wait...let me think about that for a minute." Your child will appreciate your contemplation better than your quick answer that has no real foundation.

A child who continually disobeys is in sin — sin against you and against God. However, when a parent allows or reinforces that behavior, the parent is in sin, too.

Now, there is a point where every child becomes accountable for their behavior and they cannot blame Mom and Dad for the way they live anymore. But up until that point, you, as a parent, are accountable, and God considers your behavior either righteous or sinful, based on how you parent the child. Lack of knowledge is not an excuse for sin.

I'm not just talking about preferences and things to make your life easier and your home nicer. I'm talking about requirements for righteous living. If we allow our children to live sinful lives with sinful behavior by continual disobedience, then we are in sin because God holds us responsible.

When we give commands we must be clear and consistent. When we're teaching and instructing our kids, we must be clear and consistent. We should require eye contact and verbal response and expect obedience and behavioral change the first time every time. If we'll do that, we can turn any behavioral issue or problem from a negative to a positive.

Leadership is always the problem, and leadership is always the answer. That's true for a nation, for a city, a church, and for every family. If we as parents and leaders do what is right, everything else will be cool. As parents, set the example of obedience. Do what God tells you to do before you expect your kids to do what you tell them to do.

Application of Family Covenant Truths

Please answer each of these statements/questions using Chapter 16 as your source of information:

1. "Negative parenting" means: _____

   _____

   _____

   _____

   _____

   _____

2. One example of turning a "negative parenting" situation into a positive situation is: _____

   _____

   _____

   _____

   _____

3. As a parent, my obedience to God is important because:

   _____

   _____

   _____

   _____

   _____

The "Mix" for Raising Champion Children: Teaching, Training, and Discipline

I n Ephesians 6:4 Paul says, **And you, fathers, do not provoke your children to wrath, but bring them up in the training and admonition of the Lord.**

Proverbs 22:6 says, **Train up a child in the way he should go, and when he is old he will not depart from it.** *The Amplified* translation of this verse says, **Train up a child in the way he should go [and in keeping with his individual gift or bent], and when he is old he will not depart from it.** Another interpretation of this verse is to train them up in the ways of righteousness and the ways of God, and when they are old, they won't depart from it.

We need to train our children in the ways of righteousness, in the way that they can fulfill their destiny, and be all that God has called them to be.

We have some foolish, rebellious adults running around our world today, because they were never trained up in the way they should go. "Well, my mom took me to church." I'm not talking about someone just taking you to church and telling you about God. Many people have been told about God, but they've never had an example to follow, never had proper expectations of them, and never were given moral character training. *Discipline* is the process of teaching, training, and learning that which produces moral character and moral development.

Teaching and training are both a part of discipline. *Teaching* is the process of informing, telling, and communicating, while *training* is the process of doing something with them — showing and participating.

An example of both teaching and training is a child learning to brush his teeth. "When you brush your teeth, put the toothpaste on the brush. Then go up and down and around and make sure you go all the way to the back." In this manner, you are teaching them how to brush appropriately, but that doesn't mean they know how to brush or that they are going to brush.

The *training* part of teaching a child to brush his teeth is that you go into the bathroom, get the brush and the toothpaste and say, "This is how you put the toothpaste on, and this is how you squeeze it so you don't get it all over the mirror and everywhere else in the bathroom." Hold their hand and help brush their teeth. The next morning and evening, help "train" them again. You keep helping them until you feel that they are ready to be held accountable to follow through.

Sometimes as parents we spout off some words of direction and the kids look at us and don't really know what we mean. Then we get mad at them for not doing what we told them to do. We must *train* the child as well as *teach* him or her.

The football team sits in the locker room while the coach explains, "We've got this 'x' and he's going to hit that 'o.'

We've got this 'x' and he's going to pass to that 'x.' This 'o' is going to go here, and this 'o' is going there. This is the way this play is going to go, and we'll get a touchdown." All the players nod their head. But remember, you don't win Super Bowls from teaching in the locker room. They hit the field for practice and the coach calls the plays.

The performance on the field of the locker room strategies is a more intense training activity. If the players don't get training, all the teaching in the world won't do them a bit of good.

Similarly, in a Christian environment, we have all kinds of teaching but very little example, very little participation, and very little training. People may know what the Bible says, but they've never thought of living it out in everyday life. They know what the Scripture says, but they have never applied it. "You mean, actually living by faith? Trusting God every day, like getting rid of the asprin? Like not relying on my insurance? Like not being caught up in the basic securities of the world, but trusting God?"

All of us have heard sermons on faith, but teaching on faith does not show us how to live by faith. We've got to get around people who really walk by faith, and then we'll get trained. Then we'll become effective, successful Christians.

The people who attend church services a couple times a month only get a small sample of our church. The training comes when you get in the membership class, the personal worker class, and into the home meetings, or whatever your church has to offer. Then you become a part of living and acting out what you're being taught.

If you just sit in the sanctuary, you'll see very limited results. This is why thousands come to church, but very few successfully prosper in their Christian life or in other areas of their life. Through the training is where you will see victory in the Lord.

Discipline is the process of teaching, training, and learning that produces moral character and moral development. Notice, I didn't say discipline is spanking. I didn't say discipline is making your child obey. I didn't say discipline is getting the child to do what you want him or her to do. Discipline is the process of teaching, training, and learning so they develop moral character.

Let's look at Proverbs, chapter 22, verse 15:

Foolishness *is* bound up in the heart of a child; the rod of correction will drive it far from him.

Let me ask you a question again. Why do we have so many adults who are foolish, rebellious, and unsuccessful in our world today? Because when they were children, no one drove the fool out of them. It's still in them. Little fools who don't get trained, disciplined, and corrected properly grow up to become big fools. The bad part is, it's harder to get the fool out of you when you are big than when you were small. I'm not saying it's impossible, but it's harder.

When I became an adult, I decided I was tired of being a fool, and I worked to drive the foolishness, laziness, selfishness, and stupidity out of myself. All that is part of being a fool. Now, I am working on myself, renewing my mind, disciplining myself, and doing to my life as an adult what didn't happen to me as a child. It's not because my parents didn't try. They did what they could, but for whatever reason, I didn't get it.

Discipline comes through example, teaching, and training. When children still do not obey, correction must come on one of three levels:

1. **Correct minor infractions with a simple verbal directive.** Maybe they're putting four teaspoons of sugar on their Cheerios! When you see them reaching for the sugar

bowl again, you say, "Don't put so much sugar on your Cheerios." Minor infractions call for verbal correction.

2. **Larger infractions call for verbal correction, plus some kind of action.** "Stop that and go to your room. I'll come to your room and we'll talk about it." Verbal plus action. "I want you to pick that up, clean it up, do this or that. Then we'll sit down and talk about it."

3. **Rebellious action that requires maximum correction.** As a parent, when you're dealing with correction, you have to discern between what is childish and what is rebellious. Childish behavior is spilling the milk. It moves into rebellion when you ask a child to quit flailing their arms, to sit still, and to not throw things again, and they do exactly what you have just said *not* to do.

Another example of childish behavior is when they are excited, they are running around the house, and they bump into the wall and a picture falls.

You say, "Kids, we've got too many kids in the house right now. We can't all run and play and jump, so let's play some board games and settle down." Five minutes later, they throw their cards and begin to rip and run and a picture falls down and a plant gets knocked over. Now we've moved from childish to rebellious behavior. As a parent, you need to understand the difference.

Childish behavior is part of growing up, and it doesn't need correction as much as it does more teaching and training. But rebellious behavior needs correction. When rebellion is going on and the fool is still in them, you cannot "teach" the fool out of them. You've got to drive it out with the rod of correction. If teaching could drive foolishness out, every college graduate would be wise. But many are fools because correction is needed.

You cannot "teach" the fool out of
a child. You've got to drive it
out with the rod of correction.

Along the line of correction, pain is a gift from God. If
your finger didn't hurt when you put it on the stove, you
wouldn't know that you were burning it. You might not
know until the finger was gone. Pain is also a means of
correction. In the Bible, chastisement often had to do with
the infliction of pain for the purpose of amending behavior. Let's look at several Proverbs that deal with changing a
child's behavior and setting him or her on the path to attain
championship attributes.

**He who spares his rod hates his son, but he who loves
him disciplines him promptly** (Proverbs 13:24).
"Promptly" means we're not going to let wrong behavior
slide. We're not going to be driven to the point of frustration and anxiety before we start correcting our children.
We're not going to deal with our children simply because
we're sick and tired of their behavior. *We are going to correct
quickly, help them change, and help them learn.*

We are not going to wait until they are thirteen years
old, cussing us out, giving us the finger, and walking out
the door to begin the teaching and training process. We're
going to deal with that attitude when they're two years old.
If you are struggling with a fourteen or a fifteen year old,
what they are doing now is no different than when they fell
on the floor and kicked their feet when they were two. That's
when the fool should have been driven out of them.

Chasten your son while there is hope (Proverbs 19:18).
That says to me that there is a day when the hope will be
gone. If that happens, it's up to him to get himself together.

You have a window or a period of time when you can help your child be a godly, moral person — a champion kid for Christ. But there is a time when that hope is gone, and it's then up to him to make himself a godly, moral person. That's a good word for parents who are still trying to counsel their thirty-seven-year-old kids! The hope is gone. Leave them alone and don't try to counsel them.

Sometimes we become so concerned with how our kids feel about us, and their crying or their emotions, that we don't do what is appropriate to help them learn and grow.

> **Do not withhold correction from a child, for *if* you beat him with a rod, he will not die. You shall beat him with a rod, and deliver his soul from hell.**
> **Proverbs 23:13,14**

What if we don't spank, discipline, or correct? We don't deliver our children from hell. We turn them over to hell.

Proverbs 29:15 says, **The rod and rebuke give wisdom, but a child left to *himself* brings shame to his mother.**

Have you ever seen a mother being interviewed after her son is convicted of a crime? The interviewer asks, "How do you feel about your son having murdered seven people?" She responds, "He was such a cute little kid. We always knew he had a little problem, but we never knew he would do anything like this."

As a parent, decide now that your children will not shame you when they are adults. How do you avoid this? Train them up with the rod, with rebuke, and with correction. Give them biblical, godly, moral character, and you'll never be ashamed of them.

Spanking is obviously a biblical part of correction. We should never spank, however, just because we're mad. Parents should never say, "How could you do this to me?"

Your kid is looking at you thinking, "What's wrong with you?" That is one of those immature, self-centered, pitiful, weak, dumb statements.

We should never spank just because we're mad.

Don't spank to manipulate. "If you ever do that again, that's what you're going to get." Spanking is a part of correction. It's a part of training and part of the process of building moral character into the life of every child.

Besides spanking, isolation can be part of God's correction. God used it with some of his prophets. "You're going to have to go sit in the corner for a while, Elijah, so you can get your head straightened out. Then I'll talk to you." Isolation may be an effective method of training for some children. Loss of privileges is another effective training method.

Isolation may be an effective method of training for some children. Loss of privileges is another effective training method.

Spanking is not the last straw that solves every problem. If you think it is, you're probably going to create more problems than you'll solve. It's just one of the things, along with teaching, training, isolating, and loss of privileges, that will help us to build moral character into our children.

We spank our children when all other options haven't produced what we expect in their lives. When we spank them, we do it with a paddle. We spank them two or three times, depending on their age. Then we sit and discuss why they got spanked, what they're going to change, and how they're going to respond. I have one child who, when he is spanked, is very penitent and wants to get it together. I have another who just gets mad. My response is, "Another spanking might make things better." You cannot allow rebellion to continue after the correction, because you haven't got to the result yet. The desired result is submission, repentance, and change. If the first spanking didn't do it, then we've got to continue on.

I say, "You have been spanked for this behavior. If you're going to continue to be mad, you've still got the problem. You're still in the same circumstance and Dad will have to spank again. Are you getting the picture?"

My child says, "Okay," and I say, "All right," and give time for my child's computer to kick in! I'm expecting the upgrade to come anytime! But I don't spank so I can get my frustration out. I don't spank so I can walk out of the room and say, "Next time you're going to get it twice as hard." I spank to bring repentance, to bring change in behavior, to bring correction so my child is a biblically moral person, and until I get that, I'm not done.

Some parents aren't very good at correction, because they don't want to take the time to do it properly. If I am going to spank the child, it's going to take twenty or thirty minutes to get through the process. I can't just beat my child and walk off because that's not the point. I'm not there to beat him. I'm there to bring correction and that takes time. Sometimes I find myself going, "Oh, boy, if I get into this it's going to be a half hour. Maybe I can act like I didn't see that behavior."

If we want godly, champion kids, we will follow biblical directives. The rod of correction will drive the foolishness out.

If we want godly, champion kids, we will follow biblical directives.

If we start the discipline and correction when they are young, then when they get to be ten, twelve, fourteen, or sixteen, they won't need spankings and they won't need us on their case all the time.

If we will discipline God's way, it will pay great dividends as our children grow into champions for the Lord's army.

Application of Family Covenant Truths

Please answer each of these statements/questions using Chapter 17 as your source of information:

1. A child trained in the ways of righteousness will:

   _____

   _____

   _____

2. To "discipline" my child means: _____

   _____

   _____

3. To "teach" my child means: _____

   _____

   _____

4. To "train" my child means: _____

   _____

   _____

5. An effective way to correct my child for a minor infraction is: _____

   _____

   _____

   _____

   For a larger infraction: _____

   _____

   _____

For rebellious action requiring maximum correction:

_____

_____

_____

6. Three effective training methods are:

a. _____

b. _____

c. _____

Is the *Spirit* of Your Marriage, Home, and Family Right?

I n addition to "doing all the right things" in your marriage and in raising champion children, there must be a right *spirit* in your home. If the spirit of your home is not right, then the subconscious message is, "My life is unhappy." You may be doing all the right things and are consciously saying, "I'm living the life that I want to live," yet you are unfulfilled.

Many of us grew up in homes where our parents "did the right thing." They stayed together because it was the right thing to do. They went to work to make a living. They were faithful, honest, consistent, and even went to church — maybe not every Sunday, but at least once in a while. Those are all good things, yet in many cases the *spirit* of the home was not right.

Dad came home from work complaining, grumbling, mumbling, and hid his face in the newspaper. Mom whined about Dad because it seemed as if he didn't understand or care. When Dad got mad, she would hide the kids and say, "Stay out of Dad's way, he's having a bad day." The *spirit* of the home was negative.

My parents were good people, but the spirit, the atmosphere, the attitude, the cloud that hung around the house was bad. We would have little arguments and Dad would say, "All right! That's it! No more!" The spirit, presence, attitude, and atmosphere in our home were dark.

This produces an unconscious message in a child that says, "Whatever the parents are doing isn't working." We don't consciously talk about it, but when the spirit of the home is negative, the message is, "Going to work every day doesn't work. Staying with your wife doesn't work. Acting like my parents act isn't getting the kind of results that I want."

Every human being wants to be happy. Kids are born with a desire to be happy. When they are young and immature, all they want to do is be happy. As they grow, they learn responsibility. They learn that happiness comes from things other than just playing. You have to build relationships, integrity, honesty, vision, and purpose into your life.

It's not just what we do or what our parents do — it's *how* we do what we are doing that makes a difference. Often, people do the right thing, but they do it with a wrong motive and do it the wrong way. It's good that Mom stayed with Dad, but it's bad that she stayed only for the sake of the kids. That becomes a "child-centered" home, not a "God-centered" home. And a child-centered home will always create wrong results.

It's good that Dad went to work every day, but it's bad that he sacrificed his relationship with his wife and kids to have his work as his number one priority. When he says, "I'm doing it for the family," that's the cover for his wrong priorities and unbalanced lifestyle. He did the right thing, but he did it in the wrong way. The spirit became negative and the same quality of results followed. So it's not only doing the right thing, it's doing it with the right spirit that causes the home to be good.

___

It's doing the right things with the right *spirit* that causes the home to be good.

___

Why Are Godly Kids Falling Through the Cracks and Walking Away from God?

Sometime ago Wendy and I set out on a mission to study the children of ministers. We did it because most of the children of the ministers we knew had left the church, the ministry, and the Lord. We questioned, "How can you preach the Gospel, win the world for Christ, be an evangelist, a prophet, an apostle, a pastor, or a teacher, and your kids end up committing suicide, becoming alcoholics, and living shipwrecked lives?"

Obviously, these famous and successful ministers were saying the right thing and teaching their kids the right things. So how could their kids end up like this? I believe it's because the *spirit* of the home wasn't right.

Dad would come home frustrated from trying to raise money, keeping the ministry going, and making things happen for the Lord. He'd gripe and complain about the people. He'd say, "The elders are all demon-possessed and the deacons are demons." Dad's frustration in ministry would come out on the family. Little kids listening to Dad complain didn't have the ability to discern between his own anxieties and the things that were going on, so their conclusion was, "This way of life is bad. When I grow up, I'm not going to do that. Dad comes home unhappy, Mom complains, and both are frustrated and stressed out. I don't want that."

Then Mom complains about Dad, about the church members, and about other preachers, elders, and deacons, so the kids see, "Not only is Dad unhappy, but Mom's unhappy, too."

One day the kids ask, "Why do you do it, Dad?" He responds, "I'm doing it for the Lord." They ask, "Mom, why do you stay with Dad?" She responds, "I'm doing it for the Lord." So they conclude, "Not only are Dad and Mom unhappy, but the Lord is stupid. He has asked my parents to do things that make them unhappy. You want me to follow their example and follow their Lord? I don't think so!"

Just as soon as a child in this type of situation is old enough, he or she will escape. What is the result? His girlfriend gets pregnant. He marries someone who is not even saved. He goes into a job that has nothing to do with ministry. He can't find a church in the town where he is living, because he's not looking for one!

Although Mom and Dad said the right things and did the right things, the *spirit* of the home was not right. Your spirit communicates with more than your words. You can say to your kids, "Go to your room and say your prayers!" Or, you can go to their room and say, "Let's pray, kids." This type of spirit teaches the children that prayer is good.

As another example, you can say, "Get in your room and read your Bible! Did you read your Bible today? I told you to read your Bible. If you don't read your Bible, I'm going to smack you with it!" I guarantee you, this kid is going to lose his Bible as soon as he can, because it's not only long and boring, it has become a weapon.

The *spirit* of the home communicates good or bad.

The *spirit* of the home communicates good or bad. Your words may have all kinds of insight, revelation, and ramifications, but the *spirit* is either good or bad.

When many people leave a church service, they don't remember a thing the pastor said. They just know if they liked it or not. It's either good or bad. Likewise, your spirit communicates good or bad, right or wrong, happy or sad. If your home isn't upbeat and happy — I don't mean bouncing off the wall, fluffy, and floating around — then the message is, "Our life is not working. What we are doing isn't producing happiness." If this is the situation, why should your kids follow you?

No child says, "I'm going to grow up and be sad. I'm going to grow up and be an alcoholic. I'm going to gain enough weight to hate myself, marry someone I don't like, and complain about my life every day. I can't wait until I get big!"

Instead, every child has dreams that are fun, good, and happy. He wants to be a policeman, not because he knows of the pain of police work, but because he knows of the fun of carrying a gun, driving around, and helping people. All he knows is the good part. He doesn't want to be a fireman because of the pain of carrying dead bodies out of a building. All he knows are the big red trucks, the sirens and the bells, the big hoses, and they help people and kitties get out of the fire. Kids plug into the good and the positive. If they don't see good, fun, upbeat things at home, then whatever you are telling them to do, subconsciously they know, "This is not it for me. It doesn't work."

You may love your church, but if you have a negative spirit, you will be spewing out venom, such as:

- I like that song, but do they have to have it so loud?
- I love this teaching, but don't you think the pastor goes a little over the edge?

You are communicating a negative spirit, and the negative spirit says to everyone around you, "Whatever you do, don't go to my church. As soon as you get the chance, get out." You wonder why your kids say, "Do I have to go?" Your kids don't want to go to church because of *you!*

They don't want to go to work. Why should they, because you come home from work saying, "My boss is a jerk. The traffic is bad. I'm not being paid enough. I have to park on the other side of the world. I don't understand why they ask me to do this. There's a ding-dong in the front office."

When your son is sixteen, you say, "Now son, I want you to go find a job." Sarcastically, he says, "Great! This is going to be a lot of fun. I get to be just like Dad!"

The *spirit* of the home is controlled first by the husband and secondly by the wife. The children then follow the spirit established by the husband and the wife.

The *spirit* of the home is controlled first by the husband and secondly by the wife.

Husbands, "Go All Out" in Loving Your Wives

Husbands and husbands-to-be, let me read Ephesians 5:25 to you from *The Message Bible:* **Husbands, go all out in your love for your wives....** The husband says, "I'm a quiet kind of guy and I'm withdrawn. That's just the way I am." You are going to have to change and go all out in your love for your wife. By the way, you didn't act that way at the game. And I saw you jumping and screaming on the eighth tee when you made that hole-in-one. It's not that you are quiet and conservative. It's just that you withhold in the spiritual area, but you are expressive in other areas.

Again, verse 25 in *The Message Bible* says:

> Husbands, go all out in your love for your wives, exactly as Christ did for the church — a love marked by giving, not getting.

I love that! A love that is marked by giving, not getting! Why did you get married? "Oh, she loved me. I knew she would take care of me and cook for me. I knew the sex would be good. I knew that we could have fun. Oh, I just love that woman!" Notice, *for everything you get!* It's sad to say, but you are on a collision course for disaster, because the kind of love that makes a marriage work is marked by giving, not by getting.

Husbands, go all out in your love for your wives... a love marked by giving, not getting (Ephesians 5:25 *The Message*).

When husbands complain, usually it's because they don't get what they want. "She doesn't have dinner ready when I get home. She's not excited about sex the way I think she should be. She doesn't take care of this or that." Your complaints are all self-centered. God didn't come to the world complaining about what the world did, or demanding that we get in line and do this or that before He sent His Son to be our Savior and Lord. God didn't come with a list of demands to see if we could meet them before Jesus died on the cross for us. God so loved that He gave.

My only motivation in my marriage is that I found a woman I can give myself to. I can give all that I have — my personality, my love, my faith, and everything that I have. It should be the same with you, men. In giving you will receive. You'll get everything you ever wanted, and more, if your emphasis is on giving rather than getting.

I'll tell you how to get more out of your wife. Husbands, give as Christ gave to the Church, a love marked by giving, not by getting. How does a farmer reap more out of his field? He plants more seeds. How do you receive more from God? You give more into His Kingdom. How are you going to get your wife to do what you want her to do? Give to her. You set the pace and establish the level of giving in your home. If everybody in your home is selfish and self-centered, husbands, it's probably because they are emulating you!

Now, I understand there are times when women get funky, and no matter what you do, they are not going to respond. Sometimes a wife just has an attitude! She has PMS for twelve years. But generally speaking, if a husband fulfills his biblical responsibilities, 99 times out of 100 the wife will respond.

If a husband fulfills his biblical responsibilities, 99 times out of 100 the wife will respond.

But you say, "My wife went out and had an affair." Husband, that was in response to the way you have treated her for the last ten years. Usually, when a wife has a problem, it's because the husband hasn't loved her as Christ loves the Church. When you married her, she was the product of her father. Ten years later, however, she is the product of *you!*

Genesis 3:16 says of the woman, "**Your desire *shall* be for your husband**".... So God put within the woman the desire to please her husband and respond to him.

The world talks about women being leaders, taking their place, and being more assertive, which is good. But generally a woman will respond to the leadership of her husband. If the husband does what God says, she is going to respond positively to him and she will give and love and be happy and fulfilled. But if the husband doesn't lead as Christ leads the Church, she will be frustrated and nervous. She will try to find ways to meet the needs of the children, but it is not natural. She will try to be a good wife, but it won't work because she has nothing to respond to.

So, husbands, I'm saying, *you set the pace. You lead the way.* You get the right spirit flowing into your home and your wife and kids will be fine. In the few cases where that's not true, you will have to trust God to bring a change in your wife. Still, you are to be the pacesetter and the leader. It may not be your fault for what is going on in your home, men, but it's still your responsibility to lead the way through it.

Wives, Understand and Support Your Husbands

Let's talk to the ladies now. Ephesians 5:22-24 in *The Message Bible* says:

> **Wives, understand and support your husbands in ways that show your support for Christ. The husband provides leadership to his wife the way Christ does to his church, not by domineering, but by cherishing.**

> So just as the church submits to Christ as he exercises such leadership, wives should likewise submit to their husbands.

Notice, husbands, it's not a domineering thing. The man who has to tell his wife to submit is not a good husband. There will be a natural flow and a positive response when there is a good husband in leadership.

Notice, God commands the wives to understand and support. We're talking about the *spirit* of the home. In our society, we've come through the years of the woman wanting to rise up in society, to rise up in business, and to rise up in politics. That's all very good, but because of prejudice, of the fear of many men, and of social traditions, many women have been limited in what they can do. It was right for women to say, "We need to rise up and be what God has called us to be. We need to use our gifts and talents and take our place in society." However, if you do the right thing, but you do it in the wrong spirit, you will produce wrong results. As a Christian woman, if you take the rebellious attitude and spirit of the Feminist Movement, what you are doing is right, but *how* you are doing it is wrong. You will carry this same rebellious spirit into your marriage and home.

In our church, women are leaders and influencers. They are using their gifts and talents in an unlimited way. They are pastors, elders, business leaders, and teachers. In some cases, they are doing more than some of the men are. But every now and then we get a woman who operates out of a wrong, rebellious spirit: "I'm going to show you," or "I'm going to prove to you" attitude. Although her desires are right, her spirit is wrong, and the results will be negative.

God is saying to women, "**Understand your husband.** Don't complain if he's sitting on the couch, getting bigger around the waist, and watching another game." Try to understand, "Why does he try to live his life through the victories of some athlete? Why does he watch sports rather than play sports? Why has he allowed his body to multiply itself?" Something is missing. Your anger, frustration, sarcasm, and negative putdowns will not help your husband to love you or to be the man that you want him to be.

So how are you, as a wife, going to understand the jerk? First of all, let's start with the reason you married him. If he's so out of it, what does that say about you? He wasn't overweight, lying on the couch, and watching sports until he met you! So what has happened? What happens is we want to point and blame, rather than take personal responsibility and follow the biblical command. While the husband is commanded to love his wife as Jesus loves the Church, and lead his family as Christ leads the Church — not dominating but leading — the wife is commanded to understand, "What is this guy going through? Why is he acting this way?" Once you understand, then you can help bring answers, not just add to the problems.

Wives, you really can help that guy solve the problems that make him lie on the couch, space out, and be discouraged and frustrated after work. You can help him raise up his dreams and visions again and help him go for the job he wants. You can help him live the life that he desires. You can help your husband, but you have to do what Jesus said — understand him and love him. Then you can be part of the answer rather than add to the problems. Christian wives have much more power than they think when they will allow the Spirit of God to flow through them.

Christian wives have much
more power than they think
when they allow the Spirit
of God to flow through them.

Ephesians 5:33 AMP says:

> Let each man of you [without exception] love his
> wife as [being in a sense] his very own self; and let
> the wife see that she respects *and* reverences her hus-
> band [that she notices him, regards him, honors him,
> prefers him, venerates, and esteems him; and that she
> defers to him, praises him, and loves and admires
> him exceedingly].

I Peter, chapter 3, verse 1 in *The Message Bible* says:

> The same goes for you wives: Be good wives to your
> husbands, responsive to their needs. There are husbands
> who, indifferent as they are to any words about God,
> will be captivated by your life of holy beauty.

Really, there aren't many hard-core men in the world.
There are a lot of men who act hard and closed, but they
are not. They are like a hard chocolate coating over a marsh-
mallow — they give the appearance of hardness on the outside, but they are soft inside. Scripture says though they
may appear to be indifferent to any words about God, they
will be captivated by the wife's life and holy beauty.

1 Peter 3:1 KJV says that wives are to love their husbands — be in subjection to them — and win them without a word! It's not your words, but your spirit that will
win them.

If you allow the sarcasm of the average sitcom, the sarcastic, negative spirit of some TV programs, the sexual jokes,
innuendos, and attitudes that prevail in the media today, to
be part of your home, then the spirit in your home is not
godly. You can't bring answers, solutions, healing, and

change to your husband and your children in this type of atmosphere. But if you keep the Spirit of the Lord in the home, you will be powerful and mighty, and you will lead your family right into God's perfect will.

In a recent magazine advertisement, the word "loyalty" caught my eye. I am interested in loyalty. The next line said, "Seven out of ten people who buy a GM car stay with GM. If only marriages worked this well." Can you imagine the audacity of a company that recognizes the failure of American marriages and plays on it to show that their product does better than the average American family?

Sometimes we allow the spirit of the world to keep us from solving the problems. So husbands, you are responsible to lead and to keep the spirit in your home good. When you come into that home and the kids are under homework pressures, the wife is trying to get dinner and deal with her work and other responsibilities, and you bring in an "up" spirit and a godly presence, what a difference it will make!

Husbands, don't bring the junk from your job and the challenges of the freeway into your home. But lead with the Spirit of the Lord. When there are problems in the home, bring the answers, the joy, and the peace that passes all understanding. You are lord over your own home.

Wives, be ready to understand and respond to your husbands. What a mighty team you make as you flow together as God intended!

What a mighty team a husband and wife make when they flow together as God intended!

God started two programs in His eternal existence: the family and the Church. If we will follow His plan, they will be the last two programs in existence at the end of this age, and they will work wonderfully!

To Single Adults and Teenagers:
Test all things; hold fast what is good (1 Thessalonians 5:21). In other words, don't jump into just any relationship. Don't hook up with just anyone or anything. Test it. *The King James Version* says, **Prove all things; hold fast that which is good.**

In the development of relationships, there must be a time for testing. How does this person respond when he or she is having a bad day? What happens when he or she is under pressure? You need to be with them and around them enough to watch them in various circumstances so you can see if they pass the test.

Verse 22 of 1 Thessalonians 5 says, **Abstain from every form of evil.** So you went over to your boyfriend's apartment and had dinner, watched a movie, and then you went home. Nothing happened. But try to convince the neighbors of that, because they saw you, a single woman, go into this single man's apartment and spend four or five hours there.

"Was she the one who came over last week?" they ask. You say, "What are you talking about? Nothing happened. She's just a friend from church." Then they will ask, "Do you have any more friends at your church?"

The world sees things through a certain perspective. You spend all day worried about what people think, and then you blow your witness with the appearance of evil. In the high schools, kids are holding hands, leaning and hanging on to each other, and slobbering on each other in the hallways. We tell them, "You can kiss, but that's all you can do." If you think you can start a fire and then contain it, you're stupid. But even if that's all you do, the appearance is that you are physically familiar with each other. You are too relaxed and physically involved, so the assumption is that you are sexually involved.

As a single person, you should not be going into the apartment of another person of the opposite sex by yourself. You should not even be riding around, hugging, kissing, and sitting on each other, because the world's assumption is that you are sexually involved with each other. God's Word says, **Abstain from all appearance of evil** (v. 22 KJV).

If you have been married in the past and you are now single, you need to be alert and not allow yourself to get into a position that gives the appearance of evil. I like what Bishop T. D. Jakes says: "Your fire starts much quicker."

To Young Singles and Teenagers:

As teenagers and young singles, build your relationships in groups. As a team, you can protect each other.

Guys, be strong. If your buddy is too familiar with his girl and she is sitting on his lap, pull that brother aside and say, "Hey, what's up with you? You're getting ready to ruin your witness." "Well, I would never do anything," he responds. The appearance of evil will ruin your Christian testimony. Are you getting ready to compromise your destiny? Support your friends and be there for them.

Young ladies, if one of the girls is looking for love in all the wrong places, pull her aside and say, "Your life is not a country western song, girl." Find out why she needs someone to hold her all the time. What is it she is trying to get from that boyfriend? Help each other to live victorious lives.

If each of us — husband, wife, and children — will help each other to keep a good spirit in our homes, it will cover all of our mistakes. We may do some things wrong, but if the spirit is good, then we are going to make it!

Application of Family Covenant Truths

Please answer each of these statements/questions, using Chapter 18 as your source of information:

1. The *spirit* of my home is "positive" in the following ways:

   _____

   _____

   _____

   _____

   _____

2. The *spirit* of my home is "negative" in the following ways: _____

   _____

   _____

   _____

   _____

3. In addition to what I am doing right now, I now realize there are other things I can do to bring a more positive spirit into my home, such as: _____

   _____

   _____

   _____

   _____

4. Some of the ways I can love and support my mate more
   effectively are: _____

   _____

   _____

   _____

   _____

   _____

5. As a single or as a teenager — if this applies to you — I
   can protect my relationships by: _____

   _____

   _____

   _____

   _____

   _____

To order additional copies please call:

1-800-644-4446

or write to

Christian Faith International
P.O. Box 98800
Seattle, WA 98198